PRAISE FOR THE
UNCOMMON JUNIOR High School Studies

The *Uncommon* Junior High curriculum will help God's Word to become real for your students.

Larry Acosta
Founder of the Hispanic Ministry Center, Urban Youth Workers Institute

The best junior high/middle school curriculum to come out in years.

Jim Burns, Ph.D.
President of HomeWord (www.homeword.com)

A rich resource that makes genuine connections with middle school students and the culture in which they live.

Mark W. Cannister
Professor of Christian Ministries, Gordon College, Wenham, Massachusetts

A landmark resource for years to come.

Chapman R. Clark, Ph.D.
Professor of Youth, Family and Culture, Fuller Theological Seminary

Great biblical material, creative interaction and *user friendly*! What more could you ask for? I highly recommend it!

Ken Davis
Author and Speaker (www.kendavis.com)

A fresh tool . . . geared to make a lasting impact.

Paul Fleischmann
President and Co-founder of the National Network of Youth Ministries

The *Uncommon* Junior High curriculum capitalizes both GOD and TRUTH.

Monty L. Hipp
President, The C4 Group (www.c4group.nonprofitsites.com)

The *Uncommon* Junior High curriculum is truly cross-cultural.

Walt Mueller
Founder and President, Center for Parent/Youth Understanding (www.cpyu.org)

The creators and writers of this curriculum know and love young teens, and that's what sets good junior high curriculum apart from the mediocre stuff!

Mark Oestreicher
Author, Speaker and Consultant (www.markoestreicher.com)

This is serious curriculum for junior-highers! Not only does it take the great themes of the Christian faith seriously, but it takes junior-highers seriously as well.

Wayne Rice
Founder and Director, Understanding Your Teenager (www.waynerice.com)

The *Uncommon* Junior High curriculum fleshes out two absolute essentials for great curriculum: biblical depth and active learning.

Duffy Robbins
Professor of Youth Ministry, Eastern University, St. Davids, Pennsylvania

It's about time that curriculum took junior-highers and youth workers seriously.

Rich Van Pelt
President of Alongside Consulting, Denver, Colorado

The *Uncommon* Junior High curriculum will help leaders bring excellence to every lesson while enjoying the benefit of a simplified preparation time.

Lynn Ziegenfuss
Mentoring Project Director, National Network of Youth Ministries

un**common**
be extraordinary

THE
ARMOR OF
GOD

KARA POWELL
General Editor

Published by Gospel Light
Ventura, California, U.S.A.
www.gospellight.com
Printed in the U.S.A.

Contributing writers: Kara Powell, Ph.D., and Christi Goeser.

Library of Congress Cataloging-in-Publication Data
The armor of God / Kara Powell, general editor.
p. cm. — (Uncommon jr. high group study)
ISBN 978-0-8307-5898-2 (trade paper)
1. Spiritual warfare—Biblical teaching. 2. Spiritual warfare—Study and teaching.
3. Bible—Study and teaching. 4. Junior high school students—Religious life. 5. Church group
work with teenagers. 6. Christian education of children. I. Powell, Kara Eckmann, 1970-
BV4509.5.A73 2011
235'.4—dc23
2011027506

Rights for publishing this book outside the U.S.A. or in non-English languages are
administered by Gospel Light Worldwide, an international not-for-profit ministry.
For additional information, please visit www.glww.org, email info@glww.org, or write
to Gospel Light Worldwide, 1957 Eastman Avenue, Ventura, CA 93003, U.S.A.

To order copies of this book and other Gospel Light products in bulk quantities,
please contact us at 1-800-446-7735.

Contents

How to Use the Uncommon Junior High Group Studies

Each *Uncommon* junior high group study contains 12 sessions, which are divided into 2 stand-alone units of 6 sessions each. You may choose to teach all 12 sessions consecutively, or to use just one unit, or to present each session separately. You know your group, so do what works best for you and your students.

This is your leader's guidebook for teaching your group. Electronic files (in PDF format) for each session's student handouts are available online at **www.gospellight.com/uncommon/jh_the_armor_of_god.zip**. The handouts include the "Reflect" section of each study, formatted for easy printing, in addition to any student worksheets for the session. You may print as many copies as you need for your group.

Each individual session begins with a brief overview of the "big idea" of the lesson, the aims of the session, the primary Bible verse and additional verses that tie in to the topic being discussed. Each of the 12 sessions is geared to be 45 to 90 minutes in length and is comprised of two options that you can choose from, based on the type of group that you have. Option 1 tends to be a more active learning experience, while Option 2 tends to be a more discussion-oriented exercise.

The sections in each session are as follows:

Starter

Young people will stay in your youth group longer if they feel comfortable and make friends. This first section helps students get to know each other better and focus on the theme of the lesson in a fun and engaging way.

Message

The Message section enables students to look up to God by relating the words of Scripture to the session topic.

Dig

Unfortunately, many young people are biblically illiterate. In this section, students look inward and discover how God's Word connects with their own world.

Apply

Young people need the opportunity to think through the issues at hand. The apply section leads students out into their world with specific challenges to apply at school, at home and with their friends.

Reflect

This concluding section of the study allows students to reflect on the material presented in the session. You can print these pages from the PDF found at **www.gospellight.com/uncommon/jh_the_armor_of_god.zip** and give them to your students as a handout for them to work on throughout the week.

Want More Options?
An additional option for each section, along with accompanying worksheets, is available in PDF format at **www.gospellight.com/uncommon/jh_the_armor_of_god.zip**.

UNIT I

The Defensive Armor

As we prepare to teach the next six sessions on the defensive armor of God, we would be wise to pay attention to not just the armor but also to where it falls in Paul's writings. The crux of Paul's description of the armor of God is found in Ephesians 6:10-20.

Note that this description appears not in the early chapters of Ephesians, but toward the end of Paul's letter. In fact, in the English translation of the original Greek that we use today, there are only four verses between the end of Paul's armor of God description and the end of his epistle.

Why is this important? Because it reflects an important Pauline theological paradigm. In the early chapters of Paul's letters, he tends to focus on God's love for us and how our sin has separated us from that love. God couldn't stand that, so He sent Jesus so we might have real life in the present and eternal life in the future. One of the most often quoted passages in the epistle is Ephesians 2:8-9: "For it is by grace you have been saved, through faith—and this is not from yourselves, it is the gift of God—not by works, so that no one can boast."

After Paul establishes that firm foundation of salvation by grace through Jesus, he proceeds in his letters to describe the commands that God intends for us to follow. Note that these commands—including those revolving around the armor of God—come *after* the explanation of who we are in Christ.

In churches and youth ministries today, we love jumping to the commands toward the end of Paul's letters. They seem so practical and so juicy. We teach those commands as stand-alone ideas, without the sense that they flow out of the salvation we experience through Jesus Christ. As a result, students (and adults, for that matter) end up walking around thinking that Christianity is all about behaviors—some sort of cosmic "do" and "don't" list that they have to follow. They don't realize that Christianity is first and foremost a love story—of God's love for us, and our subsequent love for God and for each other.

One way I like to explain this to students is that as we grow in Christ, we obey out of gratitude. Our life becomes a great big thank-you note back to God for all He has done for us.

Given Paul's own argument, I invite you to teach about the armor of God in the context of God's grace and our salvation. Standing every day in the armor is indeed part of how we live as thank-you notes back to God.

Kara Powell
Executive Director of the Fuller Youth Institute
Assistant Professor of Youth, Family and Culture
Fuller Theological Seminary

THE BELT OF TRUTH

THE BIG IDEA

Our best defense against spiritual darkness is a clear, undiluted understanding of what God says about Himself, Jesus, salvation and life.

SESSION AIMS

In this session you will guide students to (1) learn that there is one infallible, unalterable truth revealed to us by the one, true, unchanging God; (2) understand that this truth was revealed to us in His Son, Jesus; and (3) know that this truth brings us freedom and gives us a way to take a stand against the forces of evil.

THE BIGGEST VERSES

"Therefore put on the full armor of God, so that when the day of evil comes, you may be able to stand your ground, and after you have done everything, to stand. Stand firm then, with the belt of truth buckled around your waist" (Ephesians 6:13-14).

OTHER IMPORTANT VERSES

2 Samuel 22:31; Psalm 145:18; Proverbs 3:3; Isaiah 55:7; John 8:31-32; 17:15-17; Ephesians 6:10-14; Titus 3:4-7; 1 Peter 1:22; 1 John 5:19-20; Revelation 7:17

Note: Additional options and worksheets in $8^{1}/_{2}$" x 11" format for this session are available for download at **www.gospellight.com/uncommon/jh_the_armor_of_god.zip**.

STARTER

Option 1: Two Truths and a Lie. For this option, you will need a bunch of kids. This is a time-tested youth game that students always enjoy because it involves trying to deceive others.

Welcome students and ask them to come up with two true statements about themselves and one false statement about themselves. For example, a student might make these statements, "I've swum with sharks. I am related to Abraham Lincoln. I can eat two dozen donuts in one sitting." Choose several volunteers to stand up and share their statements. Once all three statements have been shared, ask the listeners to vote on which one they think is the lie. The volunteer will then say whether or not the statement is true or false. (You may want to start this off yourself. Students love to hear crazy things about their youth workers' lives.)

Once everyone has had a turn, point out that sometimes it is the truth that seems far-fetched and the lie that seems believable (hopefully you have an example or two of this from the activity). Life is confusing when we don't know what to believe. We want to know what is the truth and what is the lie.

Explain that today we will be focusing on truth as part of a series of lessons that center on the armor of God. Truth is not a "whatever you think is right" expression. God revealed the ultimate truth to us through His Son, Jesus. Knowing this truth brings freedom and gives us a way to take a stand against the forces of evil that rage against us. God wants us to live in a way that glorifies Him. It all begins with knowing the truth.

Option 2: Calvinball. For this option, you will need the rulebooks for several different ball games, such as baseball, football, tennis, water polo, golf, basketball and volleyball (you can get basic rules from the individual sports' websites if that's easier than books), the balls for each game you choose and a container.

Ahead of time, photocopy or print a page of each rulebook. Then cut apart the rules so that each rule is on its own paper strip. Fold the paper strips and place them in a container. The idea is to have a container with a dozen or so mixed rules. Students will draw the rules out during the activity.

Welcome students and explain that today they will be starting the session with a ball game. Hold up the container of rules and say that the game will be a combination of all the best sports games around. Ask a volunteer to draw out a paper strip with one rule on it and read it aloud. This will be the first rule of the game. Get three or four more volunteers to draw out a rule and read it. Then hand out whatever balls are needed and play the game according to the rules they have drawn. You will get a weird mesh of things that don't work well together, but encourage the students to play anyway the best that they can.

As they play, draw out a new rule every 15 seconds or so and read it aloud. Have students add that rule to their game. You can also start taking away the rules that were drawn earlier. Do what you can to make the game confusing.

After a few minutes, stop the game and ask students to regroup. Share that in the comic strip *Calvin and Hobbes*, the cartoon character Calvin invents a game called "Calvinball." His game is guided by rules that constantly change according to whether or not he's got the advantage. In other words, he changes the rules in order to keep winning. While this is humorous in a cartoon game, it is actually a frustrating experience in real life. We can't live a peaceful, faithful life when we aren't certain what the rules are.

As Christians, we believe that God who created the world gave us a means to know how to live well in it: His Word. The truth revealed in His Word is the foundation for our lives because it teaches us how to live in a way that pleases Him and glorifies His name.

Explain to the students that today we will be focusing on truth as part of a series of lessons that center on the armor of God. Truth is not a "whatever you think is right" expression. God revealed truth to us in the form of His Son, Jesus. Knowing this truth brings freedom and gives us a way to take a stand against the forces of evil that rage against us. God wants us to live in a way that glorifies Him. It all begins with knowing the truth.

MESSAGE

Option 1: Tell the Truth. For this option, you will need a sandbox with sand in it, a walking stick or cane, Bibles, a wide leather belt, a whiteboard, a whiteboard marker, a device to film people, time before the session to edit the film, and a way to show it to your group.

Film interviews with people in your community so that you can share them with your group later. Ask the people you interview the following three questions: (1) Is there such a thing as truth? (2) How do you know what the truth is? (3) Does the truth ever change? Try to get a good cross-section of people—Christians, non-Christians, young, old, men, women, adults and children. Also place the sandbox at the front of the room where your group meets so that the students can see it. Before the session, prepare to show the film to the group.

Welcome the group members and ask one volunteer to stand in the sandbox. With the walking stick, slowly draw a line in the sand around that student

as you explain that thousands of years ago an old Roman consul named Popilius was sent by the Roman Senate to stop a potential war between two powerful rulers, Antiochus IV Epiphanes of the Seleucid Empire in Syria and Ptolemy
VIII Euergetes of Egypt. Antiochus was on his way to invade Alexandria when
Popilius stopped him and delivered a message from the Senate telling him to
withdraw his armies or consider himself at war with the whole Roman Repub-
lic. Antiochus stalled for time, probably hoping to find a way around the problem, because he really wanted to invade Egypt. He already had captured many
of the cities and only needed the capital, Alexandria.

As Antiochus hemmed and hawed around, Popilius did something that
would become famous even to our day. He drew a line in the sand and said,
"Before you cross this circle I want you to give me a reply for the Roman Senate," meaning that Rome would declare war if he stepped out of the circle without giving up his war with Egypt. Incredibly, Antiochus chose not to fight and
took his armies and went home. Since that time, the expression "draw a line in
the sand" has meant to make an irreversible decision about something—to
choose something and then bear the consequences of that choice.[1]

Have the volunteer sit down, and then ask students if they have ever had
to draw a line in the sand about something. Have they ever had to make a firm
"go no further" decision about something that really affected their future? Be
ready to share something from your own experience.

Next, transition to the main point of the lesson by stating that the Bible
makes it clear that if we are followers of Jesus, we will have to draw a line in the
sand about some of the things in our lives. One of them is the idea that there
is a God who revealed truth to us through His one and only Son, Jesus Christ.
People often don't accept this idea today. They assert that truth is relative to a
given situation and that as long as a person doesn't hurt anyone else, he or she
can believe whatever truth he or she wants to believe. For us, this attitude leads
to a draw-a-line-in-the-sand decision (draw a line across the sand in the sand
box). We will either stand on one side of the line or the other. Either we will

Youth Leader Tip
The idea of satanic powers will make some
students feel afraid. Keep the focus on the
Bible and assure your group members that
while Satan is real, there is also real and
powerful protection for those in Christ.

stand on the side of the one unchanging truth or we will stand on the side of whatever-you-think-is-true-is-okay. Where we stand will make a huge difference in our future.

Now play the film you made and ask students to comment on the responses of the people you interviewed in the film. Ask for their response to the same three questions: (1) Is there such a thing as truth? (2) How do you know what the truth is? (3) Does the truth ever change?

Explain that truth is a revelation from God, which means that it is absolute. It isn't something we create or piece together. In our culture, the idea that truth is absolute or fixed is often disregarded. What is considered "true" changes depending on the situation, biases or preferences. This is *not* truth in a biblical sense. Truth is the revealed nature of God—that which is right and good and eternal. It is the foundation of everything we are and believe both about ourselves and about God. God's truth is laid out for us in His Word.

Distribute Bibles and have a volunteer read aloud John 17:9,15-17. Make sure the students pick up the main ideas by asking them to respond to the following questions:

- For whom does Jesus pray?
- What does He ask the Father to do?
- How are we sanctified (set apart for God)?
- What is truth according to verse 17?

Have another volunteer read John 8:31-32 and ask these questions:

- How do we show we really are Jesus' followers?
- What is the connection between truth and freedom?

Sum up by stating that it is the Word of God that has the power to set us apart, to radically change our hearts and to make us the people God created us to be. It is the unchanging, enduring and infallible Word of God that guides our lives. God has declared what is true. Knowing this truth will bring us freedom and give us a way to take a stand against the forces of evil.

Expand this idea to the armor of God. Invite a volunteer to stand up, and then place the belt that you brought around his waist. Read aloud Ephesians 6:10-14 and explain that this armor refers to the armor of a Roman soldier. Roman soldiers (including good old Popilius) wore some specially designed pieces of armor as protection, and while this belt may not look all that amazing, it was the foundational part of the whole armor. It was the centerpiece. The belt secured the other parts of the armor and held everything in place. During battle, soldiers would tuck their tunics into their belts so they could move around more freely.

Continue by explaining that in Ephesians 6:14, the belt is associated with truth. Truth is the fundamental weapon we possess, and it's not something we can create or make up. Truth is a revelation from God, and it is the center of faith and life. Connect the idea of truth and armor by driving home this point: Our best defense against spiritual darkness is a clear, undiluted understanding of what God says about Himself, Jesus, salvation and life.

Ask the volunteer to sit down, and then explain that God has provided "armor" for all of His followers that will enable them to face the challenges of the Christian life with endurance. This armor is more than metal and leather—it is an expression of God's character, which He works in us. And it starts with truth as He revealed it.

Continue by stating that there are a few truths that set the stage for everything else we believe. On the whiteboard, make a T-chart and place the heading "The Truth About People" on one side and "The Truth About God" on the other. Ask students to explain what they think the truth about humankind is. (This is a broad question, so you will get a variety of answers.) After a few minutes, ask volunteers to read aloud Genesis 1:27, Psalm 8:4-5, Romans 3:10-18,23 and Ephesians 2:1-5. Ask students what the truth is according to these passages in the Bible. Next, under "The Truth About People" column, list the group's responses based on the verses. Drive home the idea that humankind is a glorious reflection of God Himself, but that because of sin, people are far away from their original design. The truth is that we are all lost.

Explain that we must tell the truth about who we are. For some reason, people often try to tweak their image. They may do this in an attempt to impress others, or they may do it simply to stay out of trouble, but somewhere along the way they have put up a mask to get others to think about them in a different way. We could say these people are being duplicitous. The word "duplicity" comes from a Latin root meaning "double"; thus, a duplicitous person is someone who offers two different sides of himself or herself, usually in a way that is meant to deceive others. But God has given us a powerful weapon: truth.

Have volunteers read aloud Ephesians 2:4-7 and Titus 3:4-7. Ask students what the truth about God is according to the Bible. Under "The Truth About God," list their responses based on the verses. Drive home the idea that God is merciful. He reached out to save us because He loves us. He is the one true Redeemer of humankind who can bring us back to that original design. This is the truth that revolutionizes our lives and allows us to stand firm in our faith. We were lost, but He has saved us. We are His, and He loves us!

Go back to the sandbox. Conclude by explaining that telling the truth about ourselves and about God is the first line of defense that we have in the spiritual battle we face. We must fearlessly draw a line in the sand and stay on the side of truth as God revealed it. When we do, we will have the power to stand against anything that comes our way.

Option 2: The Purpose of the Belt. For this option, you will need Bibles. Begin by explaining that the Bible clearly teaches there is a spiritual war going on in this world: The powers of darkness constantly oppose the power of God. Ever since Adam and Eve sinned in the Garden, Satan and his cohorts have sought to destroy the work of God and keep humans from returning to Him. (If you did the starter section additional option called "Drop Off," it might be effective at this point to place the unsuccessful packing shells in front of the students—or at least what remains of those attempts. Pointing out the broken eggs further illustrates why we so desperately need God's protection.)

Continue by stating that the apostle Paul helps us understand who we are fighting and how we can take a stand. Read aloud Ephesians 6:10-18, and then lead students through the following questions:

- How are we to be strong? (*Verse 10 states "in the Lord" and "in his mighty power." Our strength for this spiritual battle isn't a matter of our own willpower or intellect or physical force. Our strength is found solely in the Lord.*)

- Whose armor do we put on? (*Verse 11 tells us it is God's armor.*)

- What is this armor, and how do we put it on? (*The armor of God is a metaphor that Paul uses to help us to understand something abstract—it doesn't represent an actual set of shiny armor descending from heaven. This protection comes to us in the form of truth, righteousness, peace, faith—all aspects of God's nature that He causes to grow in us. So, when we talk about putting on God's armor, what we mean is growing in our relationship with God so that His life is becoming greater and greater in us.*)

- Why do we put on God's armor? (*According to verses 11 and 13, the reason for wearing the armor—for "putting on" Christ—is so we can take a stand against the evil we inevitably will face. God's armor provides protection so that we can take a stand. We have a part to play in spiritual warfare: we are to oppose darkness by living out truth, peace, righteousness and faith. Living like this is what will defeat the enemies we face.)*

- Who are we fighting? (*Verse 12 states that our enemies are never people—a hard truth to grasp, no matter what your age! Satan is all about deceit, slander, manipulation and oppression. He can incite people to act in ways that feel like a personal attack, but our true enemies are not the ones who act against us, but the devil and the powers of darkness.*)

Have volunteers read aloud 2 Corinthians 4:4, Ephesians 2:2 and 1 John 5:19-20. Ask students to share what these verses add to their understanding of their enemy. As they offer ideas, draw them back to the overarching truth that there is a real spiritual battle that is taking place. Make sure they understand that standing against the enemy is an ongoing task. It's never a did-that-and-now-I'm-done type of deal. Once we have made our stand—that is, once we have committed to growing in Christ and living out His truth, peace and righteousness—we must keep standing.

Now transition the conversation to the first part of the armor of God—the belt of truth. By way of background, explain that the armor listed in Ephesians is not the medieval knight's armor that might spring into most people's minds. Many scholars believe that Paul wrote Ephesians while he was in prison under Roman guard. The armor to which Paul refers is a Roman soldier's armor, and the belt was the foundation of his entire protective gear. There are three things you need to know about it:

1. The belt was a thick leather band that went around the waist.
2. The belt had a place to secure other parts of the armor, the breastplate and the sword.
3. In addition to securing the other pieces of armor, soldiers would tuck their tunics into the belt so that they could move around more freely.

Explain that the belt is paired with the idea of truth. Ask students to consider why truth would be the first part of the armor and why Paul would use a Roman belt as a way to illustrate the role of truth in our lives. Some ideas they might come up with include:

1. The belt is worn around our center, or our core. It strengthens all the muscles that are essential for stability and strength. Truth is the center of our Christian life, of everything we are.

2. The belt holds the other pieces of the armor in place. As Christians, we cannot hope to fight against darkness or to live righteously without the securing power of truth. It holds everything else in place.

3. Soldiers would tuck their tunics into the belt for freedom of movement. As Christians, our freedom comes from truth. Jesus said, "You will know the truth, and the truth will set you free" (John 8:32). Rather than constricting or binding our lives, the truth actually gives us room to move.

State that truth is absolute. It isn't something we create or piece together. Of course, in our culture, this idea that truth is absolute or fixed is often disregarded. What is considered "true" changes based on a person's situation, bias or personal preference. This is *not* truth in a biblical sense. Truth is the revealed nature of God—that which is right and good and eternal. It is the foundation of everything we are and believe about ourselves and about God.

Conclude by stating that God's laid His truth out for us in His Word. Read aloud John 17:15-17 and draw attention to the fact that Jesus prays for protection for His people and then follows up by asking that they be set apart by truth. The Word of God has the power to set us apart, to radically change our hearts and to make us the people God created us to be. The unchanging, enduring, infallible Word of God girds our lives. God has declared what is true.

DIG

Option 1: Truth that Changes Us. For this option, you will need Bibles, copies of "Truth that Changes Us" (found on the following page) and pens or pencils.

Give each student a pen or pencil, a Bible and a copy of the handout. Instruct the group members to work on their own. The students should read the Bible verses about truth that are listed on the handout and jot down ideas that occur to them as they read.

After 10 to 15 minutes, regroup and have volunteers take turns reading the verses aloud. Ask them to comment on what they learned about truth. As you wrap up, emphasize that as Christians, the truth revealed in Jesus Christ is the

TRUTH THAT CHANGES US

Look up John 1:17 and 1 Timothy 2:7. Where is God's truth found?

_____

_____

_____

Look up Psalm 145:18 and 1 Peter 1:22. How does God's truth change your heart?

_____

_____

_____

Look up 1 Corinthians 13:6, Ephesians 4:25 and Philippians 4:8. How does God's truth change your life?

_____

_____

_____

It is God's truth that changes your heart and allows you to live in a way that honors Him. Why is it important to know where truth comes from?

_____

_____

_____

Based on what you've learned today, what is the truth about God?

_____

_____

_____

_____

What is the truth about you?

_____

_____

_____

_____

_____

foundation of our lives. His truth changes our hearts, and those changes should find expression in how we live. Truth isn't only something we understand but also something that directs how we live our lives—it is His Word alive in us and living through us.

Conclude by stating that as we take the time to know this truth through Bible study and prayer, we will be putting on the belt of truth, which in turn will enable us to stand in faith against the many challenges that will come our way.

Option 2: True or False? For this option, you will just need room to move.

To help students understand the necessity of absolute truth in their daily lives, give them a true or false quiz to get them moving. Have everyone stand and come to the center of the room. Explain that after you read a statement, they should move to the right if they think the statement is true and to the left if they think it's false. Once you reveal the answer, have students move back to the center of the room for the next statement. The questions are as follows:

- When glass breaks, the cracks move faster than 1,000 miles per hour. (*False: Breaking glass moves at 3,000 MPH. Dropping your iPhone on a concrete floor will prove this.*)
- The flames from a forest fire will spread faster uphill than downhill. (*True: So always build your dream home at the base of a mountain.*)
- A lightning bolt generates temperatures three times hotter than those found on the sun's surface! (*False: It generates temperatures five times hotter. Your grandma was right: stay inside during a lightning storm.*)
- Porcupines float in water. (*True: Although you wouldn't want to use one as a floatation device.*)
- The longest recorded flight of a chicken was 13 seconds. (*True: This is probably why so many of them end up in someone's pot pie.*)
- The electric chair was invented by a plumber. (*False: It was invented by a dentist. Enough said.*)
- A mole can dig a 300-foot tunnel in just one night. (*True: So be sure to have one if you ever get snowed in at some mountain resort.*)
- More than 20,000 birds a year die from smashing into windows. (*False: Only 10,000 die from this. A tragedy nonetheless.*)
- In Natoma, Kansas, it's illegal to throw knives at men wearing striped suits. (*True: So stick with plain dark blue just in case.*)
- A person's heart beats more than 50,000 times a day. (*False: It beats over 100,000 times a day. Aren't you tired?*)

After you've tired the students out, gather everyone together and explain that while sometimes the truth can be really strange, it is the truth nonetheless. The truth can seem silly, outrageous or even illogical at times, but that doesn't lessen the fact that it is still the truth. This is because truth isn't based on personal opinions, biases or preferences. It doesn't change because of a person's circumstances or situations. At times we make errors in what we think is true and *we change* our thinking, but truth itself does not change. It is absolute.

Guide students to the idea that unless we accept that there are absolute truths in this world (such as people shouldn't steal, or people should be honest), we will live in a world where everyone does just as he or she sees fit. Want something that belongs to someone else? If there are no absolutes, then nothing prevents you from just taking it. Didn't study and have to pass the math test? Without absolutes, it's perfectly fine to cheat. After all, who's to say whether or not something is wrong?

Conclude by stating that there is a truth outside of ourselves—a standard that exists that directs the code of right and wrong. This truth is revealed most clearly in the person of Jesus Christ. Hopefully, by this point your students will recognize that this truth comes from Christ. If they want to know the standard of right and wrong—that expression of God's own wisdom and nature—they must go to Jesus and learn from Him.

APPLY

Option 1: It's Black and White. For this option, you will need Bibles, black matting paper or construction paper, white matting paper or construction paper, several bright lights (such as a desk lamp or reading light), masking tape, several white colored pencils, scissors, colored markers or glitter pens, chairs and glue. Ahead of time, acquire enough bright lights to set up multiple workstations. For each station, tape black paper to the wall with the masking tape. Place a chair about 4 to 5 feet from the wall, place a lamp on the chair, and then aim its light directly at the black paper.

Explain to the students that because truth is absolute, it is not a matter of us *understanding* it but rather *accepting* it. If we want to fight the enemy successfully, we have to come to grips with this unchanging "black and white" nature of truth. As a visual reminder of this fact, the students will be making silhouettes of themselves.

Begin by having one student at each station sit between the chair and the wall. (The group members will probably have to move the student a little until his or her shadow hits the black paper clearly.) Once there is a clear profile of the student, have the other members use the white pencil to outline it. When this is complete, have them give the paper to the student, who will then carefully cut out the silhouette and glue it to a piece of white paper.

When all of the silhouettes are complete, have each student use a marker to write down one thing they learned during the session about truth (for example, that it is absolute, that it comes from God, that it forms the basis of what we consider right and wrong, that it sets us free). The students can write whatever they want, but encourage them to put down something meaningful. If a student is having trouble, suggest that he or she reads John 8:32. (Have a few Bibles handy just in case.)

End by recapping the main points of the lesson: There is one unchanging truth that is revealed to us by the one unchanging God, and knowing this truth brings freedom and gives us a way to take a stand against the forces of evil.

Option 2: Wall Warriors 1. For this option, you will need butcher paper, masking tape and markers. Ahead of time, cut the butcher paper into 5- to 6-foot pieces. (Note: This will be an ongoing activity for the next five sessions.)

For this option, the group members will be making a life-size "warrior" of themselves. Give each person a sheet of butcher paper, and have him or her draw *an outline* of a life-sized person. Note that there is no need for them to cut this out. Once the members are finished, tape the papers to the wall, and *voila!* You will have a wall of dedicated warriors. Feel free to have the members write their names on the papers, but ask them not to go overboard just yet with adding too many details.

Next, reread Ephesians 6:10-14 and recap the main idea of the lesson: There is one unchanging truth that has been revealed to us by the one unchanging God, and knowing this truth will bring us freedom and give us a way to take a stand against the forces of evil. Have students use the markers to draw the belt of truth on their warrior. Remind them that the belt of truth was a wide leather strap that went around the waist. It wasn't a flashy piece of armor, but it was essential. The belt held everything else in place. On the belt have them write, "God's Word is Truth; it holds everything in place."

As previously mentioned, during the next five lessons, students will be adding armor to their warrior until they have a fully outfitted soldier. Cool, huh?

REFLECT

The following short devotions are for the students to reflect on and answer during the week. You can make a copy of these pages and distribute them to your class or download and print them from **www.gospellight.com/uncommon/jh_ the_armor_of_god.zip**.

1—THE TRUTH ABOUT GOD

So, how do you put on the belt of truth? You do this by knowing the truth about God—who He really is. When you know who God really is, you will also know when something is false. When you encounter something that says it's true but is really false, you will know. You will also know how to fight against it. Look up the verses that are listed below, read them, and write down any truth that you learn about God from them.

1 John 4:8: God is _____

Numbers 23:19: God is _____

Deuteronomy 4:31: God is a _____

Psalm 7:11: God is a _____

Psalm 46:1: God is our _____ and _____

Which of these truths stands out to you the most?

_____

_____

_____

When you are having a bad day and everyone seems to be against you, remember the truth about who God is. When these truths surround you on every side, like a belt, you are much stronger. Write a prayer to God thanking Him for the truth of who He is. Mention a few of His characteristics in your prayer.

_____

_____

_____

2—THE TRUTH ABOUT JESUS

Another way to put on the belt of truth is to know the truth about Jesus. You can learn who Jesus is by studying the Gospels of Matthew, Mark, Luke and

John. Look up each of the verses listed below and write down what it reveals about Christ.

Matthew 1:23: Jesus is _____

John 1:23: Jesus is the _____

John 8:12: Jesus is the _____

John 10:11: Jesus is the _____

John 14:6: Jesus is the _____, the _____, and the _____

Which of these truths stands out to you the most? Why?

_____

_____

_____

Always remember the truth about who Jesus is. He loves you, He came to earth for you, and He saved you. Write a prayer to God thanking Him for His Son, Jesus. Use a few of Jesus' names in your prayer.

_____

_____

_____

3—THE TRUTH ABOUT SALVATION

In order to put on the belt of truth, you also need to know the truth about your salvation. There are many confusing messages in the world today about how we can be saved, but when you know the truth about your salvation, you will know when you hear something false and know how to fight against it. Look up the following verses and fill in the blanks.

Romans 3:23: "_____ have sinned and fall short of the glory of God."

Romans 6:23: "For the wages of sin is _____, but the free gift of God is _____ _____ in Christ Jesus our Lord."

Romans 10:9: "If you confess with your mouth, '_____ ___ _____,' and believe in your heart that God _____ ____ from the _____, you will be saved."

Ephesians 2:8-9: "By _____ you have been saved, through _____—
and this not from yourselves, it is the _____ of God—not by works,
so that no one may _____."

Spend some time thinking about the gift of salvation. Write a prayer confessing
your sins and thank God for saving you from those sins.

_____

_____

_____

_____

4—THE TRUTH ABOUT LIFE

A final way to put on the belt of truth is to know the truth about the life God
has given to you. When you think about your life, you might wonder why you
are here or what your purpose is on this earth. Thankfully, God has given you
His Word, where you can find true answers to your questions. Look up the
verses below and think about why God created you.

Look up Psalm 86:9. What is the purpose of life?

_____

_____

_____

Look up Ephesians 2:10. Who created you, and why?

_____

_____

_____

Look up Matthew 28:19-20. What does this say about what we should be doing?

_____

_____

_____

Say a prayer thanking God for creating your life with so much purpose. Pray
that He will give you the strength and wisdom to praise Him, do good works,
share the gospel and bear good fruit.

THE BREASTPLATE OF RIGHTEOUSNESS

THE BIG IDEA

Our best defensive weapon against spiritual darkness is the righteousness that comes from God through faith in Christ Jesus.

SESSION AIMS

In this session you will guide students to (1) learn that righteousness means living perfect lives, which is something they cannot do on their own; (2) understand that by grace God puts His righteousness on them so that they can stand holy and blameless before Him; and (3) live out that righteousness as a way to stand against spiritual darkness.

THE BIGGEST VERSE

"Stand firm then, with the belt of truth buckled around your waist, with the breastplate of righteousness in place" (Ephesians 6:14).

OTHER IMPORTANT VERSES

Proverbs 3:11-12; Isaiah 64:6; Matthew 5:16; Romans 1:16,29-32; 3:10-18; 5:5,12-20; 12:9-21; Ephesians 2:10; 6:10-18; 2 Corinthians 5:17-21; Titus 2:14; 3:3-8; Hebrews 12:5-11

Note: Additional options and worksheets in 8^1/$_2$" x 11" format for this session are available for download at **www.gospellight.com/uncommon/jh_the_armor_of_god.zip**.

STARTER

Option 1: Jumpstart. For this option, you will need a place to have a long-jump contest, some masking tape, a measuring tape, a whiteboard, a whiteboard pen, candy or other prizes and a one really impressive prize. The "impressive" prize should be something better than a half-eaten candy bar or a leftover 1982 VBS sticker, as cool as it may be—perhaps an iTunes gift card, tickets to a sports game, or keys to a new Porsche (just kidding). The better the prize, the harder the group will try.

Ahead of time, clear some space and use the masking tape to mark off an official starting line. Also mark an ending line that seems close but is humanly unreachable in one jump. The current world record for the long jump is 29'4" (set by Mike Powell in 1991), but your students will not need that much room. Just behind the ending line, place the one really impressive prize. (Note: You will be giving this away later if you choose option 1 in the Message section.)

Welcome students and choose several of them to participate in a long-jump contest. Choose one student to write down the jumpers' names and the distance that each one travels. The goal is for the students to jump (not roll, stumble, cartwheel or somersault) across the finish line and win the fabulously impressive prize. The jumpers can run up to the starting line, but at that point they must jump. The first place they touch (with hands or feet or whatever) is their official distance.

Have the jumper stay where he or she is until you can measure the jump with your measuring tape. Then have the student at the board write down the distance of the jumper under his or her name on the board. When everyone who wants to has jumped, hand out the consolation prizes and have the group members sit down. Explain that no matter how close the jumpers came to the finish line, they still fell short of the goal and failed to win the prize. Effort didn't matter. How close they were didn't matter. It's all about crossing the finish line.

Let students know that today they will be learning about the finish line of a righteous life. They will learn what and where the finish line is and what it takes to cross it.

Option 2: Weigh In. For this option, you will need a balance scale and small items of varying weights and sizes to place on it, such as toys, candy, marbles, feathers or paperweights.

Begin by welcoming students and selecting one volunteer. Ask that person to pick objects (or a combination of objects) from the table that he or she thinks will balance perfectly when placed on the scales. Once the volunteer has chosen, he or she cannot put things back or exchange them. The volunteer must place *all* of his or her chosen objects on the scale. Encourage the group to show their support through their applause and encouragement.

Give several students a chance to try to find a perfect balance. When you are finished, ask the students to comment on how difficult it was to do this. Ask them to consider what would happen if they were to weigh all the good things they have done against all the bad things. You can suggest "good items," such as going to church, helping their siblings and giving money to the poor, versus "bad items," such as lying, gossiping and disobeying.

Ask the group members if they think that the two would be equal. If not, which one would outweigh the other? Then ask them to consider what the scale would look like if they were to put God's demand for holiness on one side and their own lifestyles on the other. Would the two be even remotely equal?

Wrap up by explaining that God knows we'll never be able to put enough of our good on the scale to be equally balanced with the righteousness that He requires. We are "good enough" because righteousness isn't something we can achieve on our own. Instead, He provided a way to make us righteous that doesn't depend on us at all. Let students know that today's lesson will focus on understanding what righteousness is, how we can find it, and why it is part of the armor of God.

MESSAGE

Option 1: The Great Exchange. This option works well as a follow-up to option 1 in the starter section (jumpstart). You will also need Bibles, a whiteboard, a whiteboard marker, masking tape, markers, a Roman breastplate and an impressive prize. The "impressive" prize should be the one you used in the starter section, or some other really cool prize (iTunes gift card, other gift cards, tickets to a sports game). You can rent Roman soldier costumes from a costume store, or your church may have one in its drama department. If you cannot find a costume, just bring in a picture of a Roman soldier's breastplate armor.

Begin by reminding students that the Bible clearly teaches that there is a spiritual war going on in this world. The powers of darkness are constantly opposing the power of God, and Satan and his forces are seeking to destroy the work of God and keep people from returning to Him. God's protection against this attack comes to us in the form of truth, righteousness, peace and faith—aspects of His nature that He causes to grow in us. These aspects of God's nature are called the "armor of God."

Have a volunteer read Ephesians 6:10-18. Continue by explaining that when we talk about "putting on God's armor," we mean that we are growing in our relationship with God so that His life is becoming greater and greater in us. In the last session, we learned about the belt of truth. State that today we will study about the breastplate of righteousness.[1] Hold up the breastplate (or the picture of the breastplate) and explain that this piece of the Roman soldier's armor was made of metal strips that started at the nape of his neck. It covered his whole torso and was held in place by the belt. The breastplate protected vital organs of the soldier, such as the heart and kidneys.

Reread Ephesians 6:14 and ask students of what they think a Christian's breastplate is made. Explain that righteousness means "right living" or "right action." Right living, or living the way God wants us to live, is what protects the most vital areas of our lives. When we live the way we are supposed to live, we can stand protected against any spiritual attack and be triumphant. Ask students to consider how "right" their actions are. Without making anyone feel guilty, guide students to see that they are powerless to live a perfect life—that it is beyond their reach. Have them consider not only actions but also their attitudes, intentions and motivations.

Ask a volunteer to read aloud Romans 1:29-32. Have a volunteer list the sins mentioned in these verses on the whiteboard (greed, envy, murder, strife, deceit, gossip, and so on). Next, have students use strips of masking tape and markers to rank the sins from most offensive to least offensive. If you used option 1 in the starter section, have the group members start at the long-jump line, place a piece of masking tape on the floor, and then write the name of the sin on the tape. The worse the sin is, the farther away it should be from the prize at the finish line. (If you didn't use that option, just have them place the tape in ranking order somewhere on the floor.) For example, they might place a strip of tape near the start line and write the word "murder" on it to show that murder is a very bad sin and is therefore located far from the finish line prize.

When the group members are finished, ask them why they think people sin at all. Why can't they just do the right thing? If they tried hard enough, wouldn't they be good enough to live a perfect life? To answer this question, read aloud Romans 5:12-14. Explain that the reason people sin is because the first humans, Adam and Eve, made a choice to do what they knew God didn't want them to do. Since that time, humankind has suffered the effects of a sinful and fallen nature. At heart, we are not good, and so in actions we are not good. However, the *good* news is that while *we* cannot reach the goal of a sinless life, Christ could.

Read Romans 5:15-20. This can be a confusing passage, so read it slowly and carefully, making sure the students are tracking with the train of thought. Then, to make the point clearer, go to the starting line (or the first piece of tape) and pick up the strips one by one. As you lift up the pieces, explain that Jesus came to earth to redeem humankind from sin and its effects. When you get to the last strip, read 2 Corinthians 5:21. Share how Jesus lived a sinless life and reached the prize, and now He offers that prize to anyone who believes in Him. It is the only means of attaining the kind of righteousness that pleases God.

At this point, get the impressive prize and give it to a student in your group. As you do, explain that God's righteousness is a gift; we do nothing to earn it or to deserve it. It comes by grace though faith in Christ. Hopefully, the shock and awe of a really cool prize being handed to someone without any strings attached will help students glimpse the grandness of the gift of God.

Wrap up by explaining that this is the kind of righteousness that God wants us to wear: His! When we put on His righteous, we can stand against any spiritual darkness that comes against us. Righteousness comes from God, and it is received—not earned—through faith in Jesus.

Option 2: His Pain, Our Gain. For this option, you will need Bibles, copies of "His Pain, Our Gain" (found on the next page) pens or pencils and a Roman breastplate. You can rent Roman soldier costumes from a costume store, or your church may have one in its drama department. If you cannot find a costume, bring in a picture of a Roman soldier's breastplate armor.

Begin by reading aloud Ephesians 6:10-14, drawing the students' attention to verse 14, "the breastplate of righteousness." Hold up the breastplate and ask students to brainstorm ways in which the breastplate might have aided a soldier. What exactly did it do? Guide them to the idea that the breastplate covered the most vital organs of the soldier: his heart, lungs and liver.

Next, ask students why they think God chose to use a breastplate to represent righteousness. As they give responses, be sure that someone actually

Youth Leader Tip
Don't let any sense of inferiority turn students away from discussing the Bible, but don't let them off the hook either. Encourage them to start where they are at and then build from there.

THE PROBLEM

Read Romans 1:29-31. Write down the list of sins and rank them from only slightly bad to the absolute worst by putting each one by a number, with 1 being the least bad and 10 being the worst.

1. _____   6. _____
2. _____   7. _____
3. _____   8. _____
4. _____   9. _____
5. _____   10. _____

According to verse 32, what do people who do these sins deserve? _____

Now read Romans 3:23. Is there any person who hasn't sinned? _____

THE SOLUTION

Read 2 Corinthians 5:17-21. According to verse 17, when someone is "in Christ," what are they? _____
_____

According to verses 18-19, how did God make a way for us to be friends with Him again? _____
_____

According to verse 19, what are not counted against us anymore? _____

THINK IT THROUGH

What does it mean to be righteous? _____
_____

How should this affect the way we live? _____
_____

According to the Bible, how does Jesus' pain mean our gain? _____
_____

defines *righteousness*, which means "right living" or "right action." Guide students to the conclusion that right living is what protects the most vital areas of our lives. When we live the way we are supposed to live, we can stand before any spiritual attack and win.

Have students form groups of 4 to 5 people. Give each group a Bible, a copy of the handout "His Pain, Our Gain," and a pen or pencil. Instruct the groups to work through the handout. Walk around and offer your guidance and encouragement. When everyone is finished, gather the group back together and talk through the responses. Wrap up the message by affirming the truth that it is only through faith in Jesus that anyone is made righteous. That righteousness is what shields us from the attack of the enemy and empowers us to stand firm.

DIG

Option 1: Overcome Evil with Good. For this option, you will need Bibles, a whiteboard and whiteboard markers. Begin by choosing a volunteer to read aloud Romans 3:21-24. On the whiteboard, write the following phrases from verses 21 and 22: "from God," "through faith," "to all," "who believe." Explain each phrase to the group:

- "From God": True righteousness begins with God as He redeems us. Our righteousness is from Him.
- "Through faith": We cannot earn righteousness; we can only accept it. This eliminates any boasting.
- "To all": Just as no one is sinless, no one is automatically excluded from the gift of righteousness that God offers because of race, gender, age or heritage. However, there is one catch, and it is in the next phrase.
- "Who believe": The catch is that we have to believe. Not everyone is righteous, because not everyone believes. Faith begins with God revealing the truth to us and giving us the power to receive from Him what we could not do for ourselves. This is why Paul says in Romans 1:17 that it is "a righteousness that is by faith from first to last." It begins and ends with God.

Read aloud Titus 3:3-8 and explain to students how in verse 8, it tells us that once we are saved, God wants us to live good lives—not so that we can earn righteousness, but because we have received His righteousness. Ask students what they think a good life looks like, and then choose a volunteer to read Romans 12:9-21. On the whiteboard, list the kind of "good" they can do on a day-to-day basis.

Explain to the group that the way we fight against spiritual darkness in the world is simply to live good lives by the power of God. This means that rather than hate our enemies, we show them love. Rather than proudly keep to our own group, we reach out to those who are less popular and are in need of friends. Rather than be overcome by evil, we overcome evil with good. When we are saved, God's spirit gives us the power to live this way, which is how we "put on the breastplate of righteousness."

Close by asking students if they have ever received the gift of righteousness from God. Give them a few minutes to quietly consider this question. Then lead them in prayer as God directs you.

Option 2: For Our Good. For this option, you will need Bibles and copies of the handout "For Our Good" (found on the following page). Explain to the group that receiving the gift of righteousness does not mean that our own actions and attitudes don't matter. God still wants our lives to be continually moving toward righteousness—toward Him and His holiness—which means that we have to wrestle against temptation and sin.

Have students form groups of 4 to 5 people. Give each group a Bible and a copy of the handout "For Our Good." This is a discussion guide that will help students think through areas in their own lives that need growth in righteousness. As the students talk, be sure to walk around and drop in on the conversations, offering your own encouragement and testimony as needed.

When everyone is finished, regroup and give the group members an opportunity to share something that they realized through their discussion. End by emphasizing that God never treats sin lightly. Because He is a loving Father, He never overlooks it, excuses it or ignores it—He corrects it. When we submit to His discipline, we grow in righteousness and peace. At times this discipline may seem difficult to bear, but that is when we need to keep our eyes on the reason for the discipline: growing in righteousness. God wants us to be more like Him.

APPLY

Option 1: Let Your Light Shine. For this option, you will need Bibles. Conclude this week's session by reminding students that as Christians, we are to let the light of Christ shine to those around us by doing "good works." These works

For Our Good

JUSTICE

Read aloud Hebrews 12:5-11 and Proverbs 3:11-12. Whom does God discipline, and why?

_____

_____

_____

_____

Why doesn't God overlook or excuse sin?

_____

_____

_____

_____

How can hardship be considered discipline?

_____

_____

_____

_____

What are some areas in which you struggle to do the right thing?

_____

_____

_____

_____

How can hardships help you become more righteous?

_____

_____

_____

_____

_____

are not done on our part in an attempt to *earn* salvation, but are things we do *because* of our salvation.

Choose three volunteers to read Matthew 5:16, Ephesians 2:10 and Titus 2:14. As a group, discuss the ways the members' lives could better reflect God's righteousness. Think globally and locally! Some ideas might include standing against the injustice of human trafficking (see Micah 6:8), meeting the needs of the poor and fatherless in war-torn countries (see Psalm 82:3-4), defending the helpless students at school who are being bullied (see Proverbs 31:8-9), serving our own family (see Ephesians 6:1-3), and speaking beneficial words to those around us (see Ephesians 4:29). These are all practical ways to let God's righteousness flow through us, and they will serve as our best defense against the spiritual darkness we are facing in this world.

Close by praying together and encouraging the students to pursue righteousness in all their day-to-day activities.

Option 2: Wall Warriors 2. This is a continuation of option 2 from session 1. If you have new students, you will need more butcher paper, masking tape and markers. Ahead of time, cut the butcher paper into 5- to 6-foot pieces.

Bring out the warrior drawings that students made of themselves during the last session. If there are new people, give them a chance to draw a life-sized picture of themselves as warriors. After everyone in the group has drawn a warrior, tell the members that today they will be adding the breastplate of righteousness to the warrior's arsenal.

Remind the students about the belt of righteousness they drew last week. The belt represents the one unchanging truth revealed to us by the one unchanging God. Knowing this truth will bring us freedom and provide us with a way to take a stand against the forces of evil.

Next, have the students draw the breastplate, which should cover the whole torso from neck to waist. Across the breastplate, have students write the phrase "righteousness from God." Explain to the group how the breastplate is a gift of righteousness that God gives to us by grace through faith. It is a great gift in which Jesus takes away our sins and makes us forever right in God's sight. Because His righteousness now lives in us, we can then live lives that bring Him honor by doing what is right.

REFLECT

The following short devotions are for the students to reflect on and answer during the week. You can make a copy of these pages and distribute them to your class or download and print them from **www.gospellight.com/uncommon/jh_the_armor_of_god.zip**.

1—WHO IS RIGHTEOUS?

How do you put on the breastplate of righteousness? You put it on by being righteous. Being righteous means to be right before God. So, how can you do this? The Bible gives us the answer. Let's take a look. Read Romans 3:10. According to this verse, who is righteous?

_____

_____

_____

Read Romans 3:20. Can you make yourself righteous by following rules?

_____

_____

_____

Now look at Romans 3:22. How can you get righteousness?

_____

_____

_____

So, there is no way for you to earn righteousness by doing good things or by behaving in a perfect way. There is no way that you can be righteous on your own. The good news is that God loves you so much that He made a way for you to be righteous. He sent Jesus to make things right. When you believe in Jesus and receive His righteousness, you are made right before God. You put on the breastplate of righteousness and are protected from the devil's attacks. Write a prayer thanking God for sending His Son to make us right before Him.

_____

_____

_____

2—LIVING A RIGHTEOUS LIFE

After you recognize that righteousness is only possible through faith in Jesus, you need to begin to live out this righteousness in your everyday life. But where do you start? In Matthew 6:33, Jesus says, "Seek first [God's] kingdom and his righteousness, and all these things will be given to you as well." When you ask God to help you live the life that He has for you, He will help you and be with you every step of the way. What are some things that you feel God wants you to change so you can live more righteously?

_____

_____

_____

God will begin to change you as well (in a good way). Read the verses below, and then write down the different character traits that are mentioned.

Verse	Righteous character trait
Matthew 5:7	
Matthew 5:8	
Matthew 5:9	

Which one of these traits would you like to have? Why?

_____

_____

_____

Write a prayer asking God to give you the strength to live a righteous life. Also write about the trait you would like Him to give you.

_____

_____

_____

3—SPEAKING RIGHTEOUS WORDS

So, righteousness is only possible by believing in Jesus, Now that you know this, you need to ask God to help you use your *words* in a righteous way. Words are powerful weapons that can hurt others or help them, so we need to see what the Bible has to say about them. Read the following verses and fill in the blanks:

Proverbs 26:28: "A _____ tongue _____ those it hurts, and a _____ mouth works _____."

Proverbs 12:18: "Reckless _____ pierce like a _____, but the _____ of the wise brings _____."

1 Thessalonians 4:18: "_____ one another with these _____."

Proverbs 16:24: "Pleasant words are a _____, sweet to the _____ and healing to the _____."

What are some ways people can hurt other people by their words?

_____

_____

_____

_____

What are some ways that people can help other people by their words?

_____

_____

_____

How have you hurt other people with your words? How have you helped other people with your words?

_____

_____

_____

Do you need God to lead you to speak more righteous words that help rather than hurt? If so, take this time so write a prayer asking Him to assist you with any problem areas you have with your words.

_____

_____

_____

_____

4—BEING RIGHTEOUS

When you seek God's help in being righteous, He will begin to show you things He would like you to stop doing or start doing. When He shows you these things, He will also give you the power to do them. God's Word will also guide you in this. Read Romans 1:29-32. What are things a follower of Jesus should *stop* doing? Why?

_____

_____

_____

_____

According to Isaiah 58:6-9 and Galatians 5:22, what are things that a follower of Jesus should start doing? Why?

_____

_____

_____

What are some things in your life that you feel God wants you to stop doing? Why?

_____

_____

_____

What are some things in your life that you feel God wants you to start doing? Why?

_____

_____

_____

_____

God does not expect you to do this alone. He is right there with you and will help you. Write a prayer asking God for strength to stop doing the wrong things and to start doing the right things.

_____

_____

_____

_____

SESSION 3

THE SHOES OF THE GOSPEL OF PEACE

THE BIG IDEA

Once we have experienced peace with God, we are ready to get moving and tell others about His message of grace.

SESSION AIMS

In this session, you will guide students to (1) understand that peace begins with being reconciled to God; (2) realize that this is accomplished through faith in Jesus; and (3) realize that experiencing this peace will make them ready to share it with others.

THE BIGGEST VERSES

"Stand firm . . . your feet fitted with the readiness that comes from the gospel of peace" (Ephesians 6:14-15).

OTHER IMPORTANT VERSES

Isaiah 32:17; 53:4-5; Nahum 1:15; Matthew 5:9; John 20:21; Romans 5:1; Acts 10:36; 1 Corinthians 15:1-5; Philippians 4:4-7; Colossians 1:20; James 3:16-18

Note: Additional options and worksheets in 8¹/₂" x 11" format for this session are available for download at **www.gospellight.com/uncommon/jh_the_armor_of_god.zip**.

STARTER

Option 1: Designer Shoes. For this option, you will need digital images of shoes and a way to show them to your group. You can use all different kinds of footwear—anything from outrageous 18" platform heels to athletic sneakers. Ahead of time, search the Internet for your shoe collection and have the images ready for the session. If you don't have a way to show these digitally, just print out or copy the images.

Welcome students and ask them to stand if they own one pair of shoes. (Hopefully everyone will be standing.) Ask them to continue standing if they own two pairs of shoes. Keep increasing the number until you have only one person who is left standing. When you reach this point, ask the person to describe his or her shoe collection by answering the following questions:

- Why do you have so many shoes?
- Which pair of shoes is your favorite?
- Which is your oldest?
- Which one is your oddest?

Explain to the group that during this session they will be learning about another part of our spiritual armor, which has to do with feet . . . well, more accurately, with shoes. Show your shoe presentation and ask students to talk about the pictures. They can comment on which shoes they think are the best for running, which would be hard to wear for more than five minutes, which they would wear even if they were totally uncomfortable, and which would be worth the money they would have to pay to get them. Then ask students to think about what shoes are for and why people wear them.

Choose a volunteer to read Ephesians 6:10-15. Explain that today we will be talking about how God wants to give us some sweet shoes to wear that will aid us in defending ourselves against spiritual darkness. Those spiritual shoes are the gospel of peace. Because of the gospel, we have peace with God, and that peace allows us to be ready to share His truth with others.

Option 2: Shoe Search. For this option, you will need blindfolds, a bunch of kids and their shoes, and candy or other prizes.

Welcome students and have them sit in a circle facing each other. They will need to know the person sitting next to them, so be sure to have each person say a quick hello to the students on either side. Next, pass out the blindfolds. Instruct the group members to tie the blindfolds across their eyes so they cannot see. Then have them take off their shoes and gently throw them into the center of the circle.

Once everyone's shoes are in the middle, mix them into a huge, towering (and probably smelly) pile. Tell the students that at your signal, they are to locate their own shoes, put them back on their feet and return to their original spot. When everyone in the circle has shoes on and is back in place, they will take off their blindfolds to see whose shoes they are wearing and where they are sitting. If they are in the correct spot, award prizes to them. If they are wearing their own shoes, award another round of prizes.

After the game, explain to the group that during this study they have been learning about the various pieces of the armor of God. Ask what they recall from the previous lessons. (You can award any prizes you have left for helpful and relevant responses.) Remind the group that the armor of God begins with truth, and that this truth secures righteousness. Today, they will be learning about the third part of the armor, which has to do with feet. Read Ephesians 6:10-15 and emphasize verse 15: "with your feet fitted with the readiness that comes from the gospel of peace." Explain that the word "fitted" in this verse means designed to match the shape of a person's body. As Christians, our feet are not fitted with stinky, holey, faded tennis shoes. We have been given shoes designed especially for us that make us ready to tell others the good news of Jesus Christ.

MESSAGE

Option 1: Cause and Effect. For this option you will need Bibles, matches, Oreos, a glass of water, a towel, a Roman soldier's sandal (or a picture of one), and a brave assistant. Begin by explaining the phenomenon of "cause and effect," or the fact that certain actions lead to certain outcomes. Tell the group that some examples would include, "striking a match leads to fire," "eating an entire bag of Oreos by yourself leads to making you sick," and "pouring a glass of water over your head leads to getting wet." As you give each example, have your assistant act it out. For instance, when you talk about striking the match, have him or her strike it. When you talk about eating Oreos, have your assistant cram as many in his or her mouth as possible. Get the idea?

Transition to the next point by stating that God's righteousness always leads to peace. Remind the group that the armor of God is not some magical, mystical weaponry like they might see in a fantasy story. Rather, the armor is God telling us about His nature and how we can be protected from spiritual attacks when we take on that nature. This is why it is called the armor *of God*, and we are told to be strong *in the Lord*.

Continue by stating that it all begins with a correct understanding of truth: knowing who God is and who we are. Paul tells us that truth is just like a soldier's belt because it holds everything in place and ties everything together. Righteousness means having a right relationship with God through faith in Jesus, and it is just like a soldier's breastplate because it protects the vital areas of our lives. As we dress in righteousness, we put on Jesus' own sinless life so we can be free from accusation and blame. Living a life of truth and righteousness is the first way we take a firm stand against the spiritual darkness in this world. Righteousness, then, leads to the third part of God's armor: the gospel of peace.[1]

Remind the students that this piece of armor is meant for our feet. When the letter that we call Ephesians was written, Paul, its author, was likely in prison, so he had a lot of time to watch the Roman soldiers. Roman soldiers wore special types of leather shoes that had thick soles studded with nails. Show the visual aid you came up with (either a real shoe or a picture of the shoe). State that these shoes were extremely comfortable, which was important because soldiers often had to marched many miles in a day. The shoes were also durable and would last for years with proper care.

Ask students to discuss why they think peace would be connected with footwear. Guide them back to the Ephesians 6:15 text and call attention to the phrases "feet fitted," "with the readiness" and "that comes from the gospel of peace." Point out how the chain of thought builds in the verse: When we have our feet fitted with the gospel of peace, it makes us ready to walk out our faith.

Connect the cause-and-effect idea by explaining that righteousness leads to peace—because God acts on our behalf to make us righteous, we have peace. Peace is more than just the absence of fear or anxiety. Biblical peace includes the idea of wholeness—the contentment and calmness we experience when everything is just the way it should be.

Choose a volunteer to read Isaiah 32:17. Guide students to see the way that Isaiah parallels "peace" with "quietness and confidence." Explain that when we stand blameless before God, our relationship with Him is completely restored. We aren't anxious, fretting or frazzled; we are calm and assured because God has made us 100 percent acceptable in His sight. This total restoration is true peace.

Continue by noting that in Ephesians 6:15, Paul states that this is the *gospel* of peace. Ask the students what they think the word "gospel" means (*it literally means "good news"*). When we receive the gospel—the good news of Christ—

we experience peace. Explain that Paul outlines this process in 1 Corinthians 15:1-5. Read the passage and note to the group the way Paul breaks this down in verses 3-4 into four main events, each prefaced by the word "that":

1. "That Christ died for our sins . . ." Jesus died in our place, bearing our sin upon Himself. His death was not a myth but a reality. The nails went through His hands and feet. He literally died.
2. "That He was buried . . ." Jesus was placed in a tomb, which was sealed and guarded by Roman soldiers. He went into the grave in order to defeat the grave.
3. "That He was raised . . ." Jesus was raised from the dead on the third day by the power of God. In that act of victory, sin and death were rendered powerless over God's people. Christ's resurrection means that we can be made alive and brought into God's kingdom to live as His children.
4. "That He appeared . . ." The gospel always includes witnesses—people who have been touched by God and now are empowered to go out and spread His message, the gospel, to the world.

Explain that this is the gospel that brings peace because it is the only means of forgiveness and restoration—the only means of finding wholeness and contentment. This gospel was not a new idea, but something God foreordained before the creation of the world. Read Isaiah 53:4-5. Explain that God's plan for redemption through Jesus Christ was set in place long before Jesus actually walked on the earth. God intended every human should be redeemed even before humans were created. When we experience peace through the gospel of Jesus Christ, we are ready to go and share that message with others.

Continue by noting that in ancient times when a soldier fought a battle and was victorious, he would march home to tell everyone about his victory. So, to see a soldier walking over the hills was a good sign! It meant that the battle had gone well and that the enemy was defeated. Now read Nahum 1:15 and Isaiah 52:7-10, and explain that these draw on this analogy—the person coming over the hill was a soldier returning from the battle to proclaim the defeat of the enemy. This idea relates to the gospel, because Jesus came back from the battle against Satan and announced the victory that brings us peace. Satan and all his powers were weakened forever. We have been given freedom through our champion, Jesus. The accuser has been defeated, the justice of God has been satisfied, and we have become recipients of His marvelous grace.

Ask students why they think the order of our spiritual armor is "truth," "righteousness," and then "peace." When the students are finished answering, explain that *truth* allows us see God and ourselves correctly. This means that we realize He is supremely holy and we are thoroughly sinful. Truth also shows us that He has made a way for us to be forgiven and brought back into relationship with Him. *Righteousness* is the gift God gives to us when we believe in His Son, Jesus Christ. Righteousness cannot be earned, only received. A great exchange has taken place: God has taken our sinful hearts and given us clean ones—a new life that is holy before Him. His righteousness has conquered all of our unworthiness, and because of this we have peace.

Conclude by stating that the last thing many people do before they leave their house is put on their shoes. Once the shoes are on, they are ready to go. Ask students to think about their feet. Are they fitted with the readiness that comes from the gospel of peace? Do they have their "shoes" on? Depending on your group, this may be a perfect time to give students a chance to make a profession of faith in Jesus—to receive the righteousness that brings true peace. Be sensitive to the Lord and follow His leading. End the time by recapping the progression in Scripture that the students have learned: truth leads to righteousness, and then righteousness leads to peace.

Option 2: The Gospel of Peace. For this option, you will need Bibles, a Roman sandal (or a picture of one—search for "*caligae*" online), copies of "The Gospel of Peace" (found on the following page), and extra sheets of paper.

Pass out Bibles and explain that the next piece of armor we will be learning about are the shoes of the gospel of peace. In Paul's day, the Roman soldiers wore a special type of leather shoe that had thick soles studded with nails. These special boots were known as *caligae* and were worn by all ranks of soldiers, from the legionnaires up to the centurions. Paul would have been familiar with this type of footwear when he wrote Ephesians. Hold up the Roman sandal (or the picture of one). Explain that to the modern eye the footwear might look like sandals, but they were actually marching boots. The open design of the *caligae* allowed the soldier to keep his feet cool, and they were specially designed to reduce the likelihood of blisters.

Ask the students to discuss why they think peace would be connected with footwear. Have them look at Ephesians 6:15 again, and call attention to the phrases "feet fitted," "with the readiness," "that comes from the gospel of peace." Explain that the gospel of peace is what makes us ready to walk out our faith—to take Christ's message to the world. But how do we know what the

The Gospel of Peace

In 1 Corinthians 15:1-5, the apostle Paul breaks down the Gospel into four main events. Each event starts with the word "that." Read the passage, circle the four "that" words you find, and underline the thought each one introduces.

> Now, brothers and sisters, I want to remind you of the gospel I preached to you, which you received and on which you have taken your stand. By this gospel you are saved, if you hold firmly to the word I preached to you. Otherwise, you have believed in vain. For what I received I passed on to you as of first importance: that Christ died for our sins according to the Scriptures, that he was buried, that he was raised on the third day according to the Scriptures, and that he appeared to Peter, and then to the Twelve.

Below are the four events that make up the gospel. Your leader has assigned one event to your group. Find that event in the table below and then look up the Scriptures. As you read each passage, write down anything that seems interesting to you. Come up with a creative way to share what you have learned with the rest of the group. Some ideas would be to do a poem, skit, song or dance.

Christ died for our sins.	Christ was buried.
Matthew 27:32-56	Matthew 27:57-66
Mark 15:16-41	Mark 15:42-47
Luke 23:26-49	Luke 23:50-56
John 19:17-37	John 19:38-42
Christ was raised on the third day.	**Christ appeared to the disciples.**
Matthew 28:1-8	Matthew 28:9-10,16-20
Mark 16:1-8	Mark 16:9-20
Luke 24:1-8	Luke 24:36-53
John 20:1-9	John 20:10-20

gospel of peace is? The answer is found in 1 Corinthians 15:1-5. In this passage, Paul breaks down the gospel into four parts: the death, burial, resurrection and appearance of Jesus.

Have the students form four groups. Give each group Bibles, pens or pencils, copies of the handout "The Gospel of Peace" and extra sheets of paper as needed. Assign each group one of the four events. Ask each group to look up the Scriptures in the handout related to their event and write down anything that seems interesting to them on the back of the handout or on the additional sheets of paper. After this, the groups will prepare a presentation for the rest of the group. The presentations can be a skit, song, dance or anything else they want to create.

When everyone has finished, let the group members share their presentations and how they communicate the passages they read. When they are finished, read Nahum 1:15 and Isaiah 52:7-10. Explain that in ancient times, when a battle had been fought and won, a messenger would often run ahead to let the people know the outcome. When the people saw this messenger—"the feet of those who bring good news"—they knew the enemy was defeated and that peace would come.

Choose volunteers to read Acts 10:36 and John 20:21. Explain that the idea of a messenger returning to tell about the victory relates to the gospel because Jesus came back from the battle against Satan and announced His victory to us. Jesus and His victory brought us peace. Satan, the great accuser, has been defeated and we have become recipients of God's grace.

Conclude by stating that when we have salvation and experience peace with God, we will be ready to go and share that news with others. Jesus appeared to those He saved and then sent them out to tell others. The gospel of peace is meant to be actively taken into the world. When we get out and share the good news, we are actively defeating the enemy.

DIG

Option 1: Peace Verses. For this option, you will need Bibles, copies of the handout "Peace Verses" (found on the next page), and pens or pencils.

Ask students to pair up, and give each pair a pen or pencil, a Bible and a copy of "Peace Verses." Instruct the group members to read the Bible verses about peace listed on the handout. After 10 to 15 minutes, regroup and have volunteers take turns reading their favorite verses aloud and commenting on what they learned about peace.

Peace Verses

Look up the verses below and write down what each verse says about peace. (Some examples would be where peace comes from, what peace means in your daily life, how long peace lasts . . . stuff like that.)

Isaiah 26:3

_____

_____

_____

John 14:27

_____

_____

Romans 15:13

_____

_____

_____

Philippians 4:7

_____

_____

_____

Colossians 3:15

_____

_____

_____

Now go back and circle two verses that really stood out to you. Reread your verses, and in the space below write down one specific thing that verse shows you about peace.

My Peace Verse 1:

_____

_____

_____

My Peace Verse 2:

_____

_____

_____

Emphasize to the students that the kind of peace God has given to us in Christ is not dependent on our circumstances. Nothing can overcome the peace that He shares with us because it is part of His own nature. When we daily take the time to know Him, His peace will make us ready to stand in faith against the many things that will challenge us.

Option 2: *Shalom*. For this option, you will need two identical, framed mirrors (such as the kind kids use in their lockers), a hammer, glue, a towel and a table.

Explain to the students that the kind of peace God gives us is not an emotional feeling. It is part of His very nature, which He shares with us. It is a peace that comes through righteousness.

Have everyone say aloud the Hebrew word for peace: *shalom*. Explain that *shalom* means much more than just everyone agreeing about what toppings to put on a pizza—more than just being quiet—it also carries the idea of complete wholeness, where every part of us is put together in perfect harmony. *Shalom* can be defined by words such as "completeness," "safety," "health," "prosperity," "contentment" and "friendship." This is the peace that God gives us.

Hold up one of the mirrors and explain how it represents *shalom* because it is a whole or complete object. However, before we were even born, this wholeness was shattered because of sin. Lay the mirror down on the table, cover it with the towel, and use the hammer to break it into pieces. Carefully hold the shattered mirror up for students to see. Continue by explaining how sin destroyed the wholeness that God intended for us, which is why anxiety and fear—the opposite of peace—often make us feel like we are broken up inside. We feel just like this mirror looks when our peace and wholeness are broken.

Ask the students to suggest ways people try to find peace and wholeness today. As they begin to answer, try to glue some of the bigger pieces back into the frame. When the group has finished, hold up your best efforts at repairing the mirror. Explain to the group that the problem with our best efforts is that they never make us whole again. They can never give us true *shalom*.

Now choose a volunteer to read aloud Ephesians 2:14 and Colossians 1:20. Explain that *shalom* can only be given to us by Jesus. Hold up the unbroken mirror, and explain that when we come to faith in Christ, He takes away our old, broken, peace-less heart and gives us His *shalom*. He makes us whole again the way God intended.

End this part of the session by reminding the group how experiencing this kind of peace is what makes them ready to share the good news with others.

When God has put our lives back together and made us whole, we will naturally want to share this with those around us. This is part of the way we stand against spiritual darkness—we live lives of *shalom*.

APPLY

Option 1: Prayer Circles. For this option, you will need a Bible and time to pray. Reread Ephesians 6:10-15. Explain to the group that spiritual warfare can take many forms in our day-to-day lives, but our best defense is to live lives of truth, righteousness and peace. These attributes come from God, so their strength is in Him—and that means victory!

Instruct students to form small prayer circles. Ideally, you should have one adult leader with each group. Ask students to share circumstances in their lives that they are worried about with their group members. Have each group pray for those in the circle. Once this is finished, bring everyone back to the main group. Pray that God would bring each student wholeness, peace and opportunities to share the gospel of peace with someone else.

Close by reminding the group members that when they invest time in Bible study and prayer, they will be armed to win the spiritual battles around them. As their relationship with God grows, they will have the strength and boldness to resist the enemy. This is how they put on the armor of God and find the grace to stand!

Option 2: Wall Warriors 3. This is a continuation of option 2 from session 1 and session 2. If you have new students, you will need more butcher paper, masking tape and markers. Ahead of time, cut the butcher paper into 5- to 6-foot pieces.

Conclude this week's session by having the group members continue to create their life-sized "warrior." This week, they will be drawing shoes made from the gospel of peace. Reread Ephesians 6:10-15 if needed, and remind the group members of the main idea: the gospel brings us back to God, which gives us lasting and perfect peace. Have students add shoes to their life-sized warriors, and then across the shoes, have them write the phrase "gospel of peace."

End by reminding the group how the good news of reconciliation with God brings us peace that cannot be taken away by anyone. This confidence motivates us to get to our feet and share His grace with others. Close in prayer.

REFLECT

The following short devotions are for the students to reflect on and answer during the week. You can make a copy of these pages and distribute them to your class or download and print them from **www.gospellight.com/uncommon/jh_the_armor_of_god.zip**.

1—OBSTACLES TO PEACE

In order to put on the shoes of peace, you need to trust God and receive His peace. However, to do this, you may need to identify some things in your life that could prevent you from being peaceful. Do that right now—list five things in your life that cause you stress and keep you from being peaceful.

1. _____
2. _____
3. _____
4. _____
5. _____

When Jesus announced to His disciples that He would be leaving them, they certainly had reason to worry. However, Jesus told them that He would not leave them alone—He would send the Holy Spirit to give them peace. Look up John 14:27 and write down what Jesus said to them.

_____
_____
_____

Notice that this verse gives the disciples two tasks. First, they were not to let their hearts be troubled. Second, they were not to be afraid. Fear and worry are just two of the many things that stop us from being peaceful! Look back at the five stressful things you listed above. Are any of them related to fear? To worry? Any time you worry, you are not completely trusting in God. Write a prayer asking God to help you trust Him instead of allowing worry and fear to steal your peace.

_____
_____
_____

2—PEACE THROUGH PRAYER

True peace—the kind that Christ gives—can help you stay true to God and tell others about how good He has been to you. However, putting on the shoes of peace will require you to do something: let go of your fear, stress and worry and *trust God.* Look up Philippians 4:4-7. What does God want you to do?

_____

_____

_____

In these verses, Paul was telling believers how to stop being anxious. Every time they faced something that made them feel worried, they could tell God about it and ask for help! The same is true today. When we take our worries to God and ask for help, He promises to give us peace that is so amazing we can't even explain it. Try this out today. Write down two things (big or small) that worried you today. Under each one, write a prayer asking God for strength and peace to deal with that situation.

Problem #1: _____

My prayer: _____

_____

_____

Problem #2: _____

My prayer: _____

_____

_____

3—HAVING PEACEFUL RELATIONSHIPS

How do you get peace from God? By asking Him for it and by believing He will give it to you! What effect will God's peace have on you? It will make you trust Him more. When this happens, you will be able to share your peace with others. This is what the Bible calls being a peacemaker. Look up Matthew 5:9. What does Jesus say will happen to you when you become a peacemaker?

_____

_____

_____

Look up the following verses. After reading each verse, write down what it says you need to do to be a peacemaker and have peaceful relationships.

Scripture	What to do to be a peacemaker
Romans 12:18	
James 3:16-18	
Hebrews 12:14	

Is there any relationship in your life that could be more peaceful? If so, ask God to give you His peace for that situation.

4—SPREADING THE GOSPEL OF PEACE

Christ died so that you could have peace with God. But it doesn't end there! Once you receive God's peace, you need to give God thanks for it and share it with others. Look up the following passages and fill in the blanks.

Romans 5:1-2: "Since we have been justified through _____, we have _____ with God through our Lord Jesus Christ, through whom we have gained access by faith into this _____ in which we now stand."

Matthew 28:19-20: "Therefore go and make _____ of all nations, baptizing them in the name of the Father and of the Son and of the Holy Spirit, and _____ them to obey everything I have commanded you."

As you tell others about Jesus, they will learn about the peace that comes from being right with God. Who do you know who needs that kind of peace today? Write down the names of three people.

1. _____
2. _____
3. _____

Today, ask that God will give you opportunities to share the gospel of peace with these individuals.

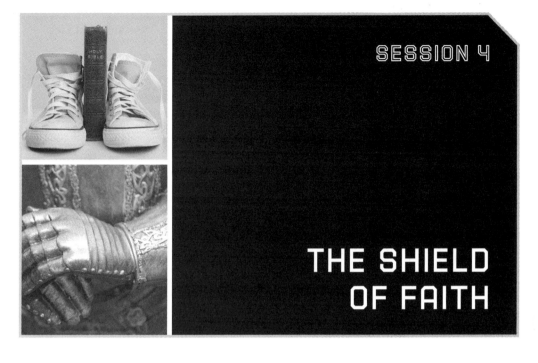

THE SHIELD OF FAITH

THE BIG IDEA

We use the shield of faith when we declare our belief in God.

SESSION AIMS

In this session, you will guide students to (1) realize that the devil is constantly trying to tempt them to doubt the message of the gospel; (2) understand that they raise the shield of faith when they declare their trust in Jesus; and (3) believe that faith in Jesus can lead them to victory in any difficulty.

THE BIGGEST VERSE

"In addition to all this, take up the shield of faith, with which you can extinguish all the flaming arrows of the evil one" (Ephesians 6:16).

OTHER IMPORTANT VERSES

Genesis 15:1; 2 Samuel 22:3,31,36; Psalm 115:9-11; Proverbs 30:5; Mark 12:30; Romans 10:13; Hebrews 11:1; James 2:14-26; 1 Peter 4:10; Revelation 21:4

Note: Additional options and worksheets in 8$^1/_2$" x 11" format for this session are available for download at **www.gospellight.com/uncommon/jh_the_armor_of_god.zip**.

STARTER

Option 1: Dart Tag. For this option, you will need Nerf dart guns, eye protection and lots of Nerf darts for each student in the group.

Welcome the group members and then divide them into two teams. Hand out the Nerf dart guns and darts for a little game of dart tag. If you don't have enough guns for everyone, allow the teams to pick some of their members to be "obstacles" they can hide behind. Each team's goal will be to eliminate the members of the other team by tagging them with a dart. Tell the members that targeting other players' faces is strictly off limits.

Once someone is shot, that person must sit down immediately and give his or her gun to you or another leader. After this, the person becomes an "obstacle." The student may shield the other players that are still in the game, but he or she cannot move from that spot. Hopefully, as students are tagged, the room will become strewn with "obstacles" that will enable the remaining players to stay alive longer. When the last player is standing, declare him or her the winner.

Have everyone come back to the main group. Explain that today's lesson is on the fourth piece of God's armor: the shield of faith. When our enemy attacks us, we need to be able to protect ourselves from harm. Faith in God acts as a shield in our fight against spiritual darkness. This is another way we can stand against the enemy.

Option 2: Trust Me? For this option, you will need trusting kids. Welcome the students and ask them what they think it means to have faith. Let students offer their ideas, and then follow up by asking when they feel it is easy to have faith and when they feel it is hard. See if there are a few students who are willing to describe a time when they had faith and what happened because of it (adding your own stories is always a bonus!).

Explain that this is exactly what the meaning of faith is: to rely on someone and trust him or her. This can be difficult for us at times, because to trust someone else means that we must let go of an area of control and rely on that person to take care of things. To illustrate this, have each student pair up with someone he or she trusts. Instruct the pairs to take turns doing the good ol' "trust fall," where one person falls backward into the arms of the other. Let the pairs take turns doing this a couple times, and then gather everyone back to the main group to continue the discussion.

Ask students to describe what it felt like as they *began* to fall backward. Explain that for most people, the first second or two is the scariest because it's the moment when they give up control. Next, ask students to think about why they trusted their partner. What made it easy to trust him or her? What made it hard to trust?

Transition to the lesson by explaining that today they will be learning about the fourth piece of the armor of God: the shield of faith. Have a volunteer read Ephesians 6:16. Explain that the shield of faith is another way God has provided for us to stand against the spiritual enemy we face.

MESSAGE

Option 1: Faith Object Lesson. For this option, you will need Bibles, a whiteboard, whiteboard markers, a six-foot length of rope with a grappling hook at one end, a wedding ring (or something that looks like one), a package of seeds and a true-to-size Roman shield. (Note: If you can't find a shield, you can make one out of cardboard. A shield was about four feet by two feet and was covered in leather.)

Before getting into the specifics about the shield of faith, review the following points of what the students have learned so far:

1. We are to "be strong in the Lord and in his mighty power" (Ephesians 6:10). Our own strength is insufficient to enable us to stand against spiritual darkness. We must be strong in the Lord.
2. We are to "put on the full armor of God" (Ephesians 6:11). God's armor isn't a magical sci-fi or fantasy weapon. It is a specific aspect of God's character that He gives to us and grows in us.
3. We wrestle against "the spiritual forces of evil in the heavenly realms" (Ephesians 6:12). We have a real enemy who is constantly trying to draw us away from a vibrant relationship with God.
4. Once we put on the armor of God, we are commanded to "stand firm" against darkness (Ephesians 6:13-14). This is a battle we will fight for the rest of our lives. It will require a constant effort and commitment on our part.
5. The specific pieces of armor we've covered so far are the belt of truth, the breastplate of righteousness, and the gospel of peace (see Ephesians 6:14-15). Each of these pieces of armor reflects an aspect of God's nature.

Have a volunteer read aloud Ephesians 6:10-16. Explain to the group that the fourth piece of God's armor is a shield. This shield can actually stop the "flaming arrows" of the enemy that come our way, enabling us to stay standing even when the fighting gets fierce.

Hold up the Roman shield and state that this was a large, oblong shape—kind of like a door.[1] Typically, it was made of wood and covered with animal skins. Sometimes the soldiers soaked the shields in water to defend themselves against arrows that had been dipped in pitch and lit on fire. The shield was an important asset for a soldier, because it was his first line of defense. It deflected the enemy's attack before it could do any harm. Thus, when Paul says in the Bible that our faith is like a shield, he is saying that faith is our first line of defense against the spiritual darkness we face as followers of Jesus. It is what God has given us to defuse—and even completely stop—the attack of the enemy.

Continue by stating that spiritual attacks are the devil's constant attempts to cause us to doubt and to move us away from Jesus. The devil does not want us to be dependent on God or to hope in His promises. Raising the shield of faith means that we trust and rely on Jesus despite the struggles we face. Of course, there are a few things that we need to know about faith to use the shield effectively.

First, *faith is anchored to strength.* Our culture often encourages us to have faith in many things, but real faith is more than just positive thinking. Real faith means being able to rely on someone else to do what he or she has promised to do. Ask the students to list some things in which they think people today place their faith. You can list these on the whiteboard as they give their answers.

Next, choose a volunteer to read Hebrews 11:1. Explain that the Bible teaches that faith is having "confidence in what we hope for." Ask the students to consider how the things listed on the whiteboard bring people the confidence to keep hoping. Most likely, they will find that what our culture means by faith is not the same as what God means by faith. Explain that most of what passes for faith is actually a weak attempt to keep a positive attitude. This is because the strength of our faith is directly linked to those things in which we put our faith. Having faith in beauty, reason, ambition, people, abil-

Youth Leader Tip

When conducting discussions, be sure to watch out for those students who are quiet and encourage them to get them involved. Build an atmosphere of acceptance of ideas, and don't let anyone leave feeling "stupid."

ities or anything else cannot generate true faith in us, because these things are all finite, fallible and imperfect.

Hold up the rope with the grappling hook. Explain that in one way this rope is like hope. It is something we can hold on to and something that we can grasp. However, unless the rope is secured to an object that is strong and stable, it isn't going to be of any use to us, because it will not hold us. Faith, then, is being sure of what we have placed our hope in—what we are relying on. When we put our faith in things that are passing—the things listed on the whiteboard—we will find that they are not strong enough to hold us. At some point, they will break and we will come crashing down. However, when we put our faith in Christ, we can "hook" on to a true source of strength. This does not mean that we will never doubt, but when we do, we will still have an unshakable confidence because our faith rests in the One who is truly able.

A second point about faith is that it is *a relationship*. Hold up the wedding ring and explain how faith is not a one-time event but rather an ongoing relationship of trust with Jesus. When a couple gets married, they commit themselves to years of relationship with the other person. They don't get married and then go on living the same way they did before. It is the same with our faith in Jesus. Although there is one moment of faith when we receive salvation and start our journey with Christ, there is also a lifetime of learning to love Him and serve Him well. Our faith sets us on a new course and permanently changes the way we live. Our lives are now centered on Jesus.

Explain that sometimes spiritual attacks will come that will try to draw our hearts away from Christ. Just like the serpent in the Garden of Eden, Satan will tempt us to believe that God is not good, that His Word is not true, and that we know better than He does. When that happens, we need to remember that we are called to a life of faithfulness to God.

Finally, we need to realize that *faith leads to action*. Explain that genuine, biblical faith always leads to actions that show others how much Jesus loves them. Read James 2:14-26 and state that in this passage, James gives specific examples of people whose honest trust in God led them to do great things for Him. Ask students to discuss both Abraham's and Rahab's stories. You might want to phrase the questions this way: "How does the story we read about Abraham show that his true faith in God led to an action? What was that action? How does the story of Rahab show that her true faith led to an action? What was that action?"

Next, hold up the package of seeds. Explain that within each of these seeds there is the potential for a flower to grow. We can show the seeds, brag about how many we have and talk about the beautiful garden we are going to own in the spring, but until we get busy cultivating the dirt and planting the seeds, it won't make any difference. Likewise, we can say that we have faith in Jesus, but we shouldn't stop there. Genuine, biblical faith will compel us to express it to others.

Connect faith back to the armor of God by explaining how the shield of faith is not like a sci-fi force field; we don't muster up positive thoughts to resist the devil's temptations. Rather, our shield is a confident trust in and reliance on Jesus, which leads us to actions that help others. This kind of faith will quell every attack the enemy throws at us because we are asserting the power and authority of the sovereign King. The temptation to doubt will be conquered when we raise this shield of faith and hold to our conviction that Jesus is Lord over all.

Option 2: Faith by Example. For this option, you will need Bibles. Begin by reviewing some of the basic information on the armor of God that you have covered so far: (1) We are to "be strong in the Lord and in his mighty power" (Ephesians 6:10); (2) we are to "put on the full armor of God" (Ephesians 6:11); (3) we wrestle against "the spiritual forces of evil in the heavenly realms" (Ephesians 6:12); (4) we are commanded to "stand firm" against darkness (Ephesians 6:13-14); and (5) we do this by equipping ourselves with the belt of truth, the breastplate of righteousness, the gospel of peace and the shield of faith (see Ephesians 6:14-16).

Also explain that Roman shields were about four feet by two feet and were made out of wood covered with animal skins. When the soldiers were attacked, they would raise these shields and trust that they would protect them from their enemy's weapons. By doing this, they were able to advance forward in the midst of a battle. A successful battle tactic the Roman soldiers employed was to move close together and use their shields to form a shell that covered the group. This formation, called a *testudo* (which means "tortoise"), made it possible for the whole group to bulldoze forward without being harmed.

Explain to the group that the shield of faith represents our trust that God will faithfully lead us through any difficult circumstance. No matter what the actual situation, the ultimate aim of the enemy is to draw our hearts away from dependence on God. The shield of faith is our refusal to stop trusting in Jesus—even when everything around us and in us says to do so. Today, the group is going to examine some stories from the Bible in which people had to use their shield of faith. Divide the students into three groups and assign the groups the following passages:

- Genesis 22:1-18: Abraham offers Isaac as a sacrifice
- Daniel 3:1-30: Shadrach, Meshach and Abednego
- Matthew 4:1-11: Jesus in the desert

Have each group read their assigned passage. When they have finished reading, they will need to figure out the story of faithfulness—who was being faithful, how that person was being faithful, why he or she was being faithful, and so forth. Once they have done this, they will need to create a skit that tells the story and then present it to the whole group. After the groups have finished their skits, draw out the idea that faith in God leads to (sometimes radical) obedience. Genuine faith refuses to take God as anything less than the perfect, all-power, infallible King of everything.

Remind the group members that the shield of faith represents our confident trust in and reliance on Jesus. This kind of faith will stop the attacks that the enemy throws our way because we are acting in the power and authority of our sovereign King.

DIG

Option 1: Hall of Faith. For this option, you will need Bibles, a whiteboard and whiteboard markers. Ahead of time, draw a chart on the whiteboard. You will need to have three columns. Label the first column "Scripture," the second column "name," and the third column "their act of faith."

Begin by explaining that faith in Jesus has given people courage to accomplish many amazing things and to face difficult circumstances. Choose a volunteer to write on the whiteboard, and then choose another volunteer to read aloud the passages in Hebrews 11 indicated in the table below. As one student reads, have the other fill in the names on the whiteboard and acts of faith mentioned. Be aware that verses 32-34 are laid out differently and will probably have to be listed as a group.

Scripture	Name	Their act of faith
11:4	Abel	Offered a better sacrifice and was declared righteous
11:5-6	Enoch	Pleased God and did not face physical death
11:7	Noah	Saved his family

Scripture	Name	Their act of faith
11:8-9, 11,17	Abraham	Followed God to a new land, trusted God would give him a child, offered Isaac as a sacrifice
11:21	Jacob	Blessed Joseph's sons
11:22	Joseph	Spoke about the Exodus and gave instructions about his bones
11:24-28	Moses	Chose to be an Israelite, left Egypt, persevered, kept the Passover
11:31	Rahab	Welcomed the spies
11:32-34	Gideon and others	Conquered kingdoms, administered justice, gained what was promised, shut mouths of lions, quenched flames, escaped death, routed armies

Once the group members have worked through these verses, ask them which people stood out to them and why. Help them to see the connection between how a person's faith becomes an act of faith.

Conclude by reading verse 39. Ask students if they have experienced times when they felt as if they had faith that something was going to happen but never saw God do it. How did this affect them? Were they tempted to doubt God? Explain that faith in Jesus doesn't mean we are guaranteed to receive every blessing in this life. We may not receive some blessings until we get to heaven. The important thing is that we have faith in God regardless of what happens. We can be assured that faith in Jesus will lead to ultimate victory.

Option 2: God's Faithful Promises. For this option, you will need Bibles, copies of the handout "God's Faithful Promises" (found on the next page), and pens or pencils. Read Hebrews 11:1 and remind the group that faith is directly linked to hope. One way we often explain hope is to think of it as something we wish might happen—kind of like, "I *hope* this happens." Hope that comes from God is different. While our hopes are wishes that may or may not happen, hope from God is always rooted in His greater purpose and always happens in His time. God's Word reveals many promises to us, and these promises can inspire godly hope.

Have students pair up. Pass out Bibles, copies of "God's Faithful Promises," and pens or pencils. Have the pairs work together to complete the handout.

God's Faithful Promises

God has made promises to you, and He always keeps His word. Look up the following verses to find out how God is faithful to you:

Psalm 46:1
Romans 10:13
1 Corinthians 10:13
1 Thessalonians 5:23-24

1 Peter 1:3-4
1 John 1:9
Jude 1:24
Revelation 21:4

From the verses you just read, what are some ways that God is faithful to you?

_____
_____
_____
_____
_____

When you look at the ways that God is faithful to you, how does it make you feel about God? How does it make you feel about yourself? Why?

_____
_____
_____
_____
_____

Which promise that you read encourages you the most right now? Why?

_____
_____
_____
_____
_____
_____

When everyone is finished, regroup and share responses. Emphasize how the promises of God are not like a list of ice cream flavors that we can pick and choose as we see fit. Though we benefit from His promises, they are an expression of His glory. God's promises demonstrate His faithfulness. When we experience them, they cause us to respond with faith-filled gratitude.

APPLY

Option 1: The Biggest Lie. For this option, you will just need time to pray.

End today's session by helping the group members see that the worst kind of "fiery darts" that Satan shoots at them is not the temptation to *reject* God but rather the subtle temptation to live *independent* from God. Our culture is constantly pushing the idea that we have all we need and are self-sufficient. It tells us that with a little "elbow grease," we can achieve anything. This mantra oozes from our society's music, literature and movies. For this reason, it is very difficult to maintain a different mindset from what our culture is continually telling us. So we need to pray!

Have the students spend some time in prayer, confessing the areas of their lives where they have been relying on their own strength, wisdom or abilities to make it through. Encourage them to ask for God's help so they can begin placing their trust in Jesus as the object of their faith. As they do this, vigilantly assure them that they are important apart from their abilities or inabilities. Help them see that dependence on God is a valiant act of faith. It will take a lot of courage to put their lives in the hands of someone else—especially Someone they have never seen—but the rewards are eternal.

Close by stating that trust is how they can show God love and respect. It is also another way we can push back the spiritual darkness surrounding us.

Option 2: Wall Warriors 4. This is a continuation of option 2 from sessions 1–3. If you have new students, you will need more butcher paper, masking tape and markers. Ahead of time, cut the butcher paper into 5- to 6-foot pieces. Also, you will need some additional paper cut into shield shapes.

Tell the students they will be adding the next piece of spiritual armor to their wall warriors: the shield of faith. Hand out the paper shields. You want to have students tape their shields up next to their wall warriors, as the shields will almost be the size of a body. Across the shield, have students write the phrase "relying on Jesus." Reread Ephesians 6:10-16, and conclude by reminding the group members that the shield of faith is their first line of defense against the enemy.

REFLECT

The following short devotions are for the students to reflect on and answer during the week. You can make a copy of these pages and distribute them to your class or download and print them from **www.gospellight.com/uncommon/jh_ the_armor_of_god.zip**.

1—THE FAITHFULNESS OF GOD

In order to use the shield of faith, you have to trust that God will be faithful to you. Your trust in Him is a powerful weapon that will help you fight the devil. The following verses focus on God's faithfulness. Look up the verses, read them, and write down one thing that each reveals about God.

1 Samuel 15:29: God does not _____ or _____ His _____.
Deuteronomy 7:9: God is _____ and keeps His _____.
Deuteronomy 32:4: God is the _____.
Psalm 111:5: God _____ His covenant forever.

Think about the verses you just read. How would your life change if you truly believed God would always be faithful to you?

_____
_____
_____

Write a prayer thanking God for who He is. Ask Him to help you trust that He will always be faithful to you.

_____
_____
_____

2—BEING A FAITHFUL FOLLOWER

Because God is always faithful to you, you also need to be faithful to Him. Your faithfulness to God is a powerful weapon that will help you fight the devil. Look up the following verses and write them down. Circle the words in the verses that tell you what you need to be doing because of God's faithfulness.

Hebrews 10:23

_____

_____

_____

Proverbs 28:20

_____

_____

_____

1 Corinthians 4:2

_____

_____

_____

Galatians 5:22

_____

_____

_____

Write a prayer asking God for the strength to be faithful to Him every day of your life.

_____

_____

_____

3—LOVE GOD WITH ALL YOUR . . .

In order to be faithful to God, you need to love and serve Him with all that you are. In Mark 12:30, Jesus said, "Love the Lord your God with all your heart and with all your soul and with all your mind and with all your strength." Think about this verse for a minute. What are some ways you can use your heart (emotions) to love God?

_____

_____

_____

What are some ways you can use your soul (the real you that may or may not be shown to other people) to love God?

_____

_____

_____

What are some ways you can use your mind (thoughts) to love God?

_____

_____

_____

_____

What are some ways that you can use your strength (what you are good at) to love God?

_____

_____

_____

_____

Write a prayer asking God for the strength to be faithful in all areas of your life.

_____

_____

_____

4—PRACTICING FAITHFULNESS

In order to use the shield of faith, you have to live a faithful life. How do you do this? Read the following verses and fill in the blanks below:

Joshua 1:8: We can be faithful to God by spending time reading and _____ on (thinking about and memorizing) His Word.

James 5:13: We can be faithful to God by spending time in _____ and by singing songs of _____ to God.

1 Peter 4:10: We can be faithful to God by using our _____ to _____ others.

Think about the verses you just read. Do you spend time reading and memorizing God's Word each day? Why or why not?

_____

_____

_____

_____

_____

When God answers your prayers or blesses you in some way, do you thank Him for it? Why or why not?

_____

_____

_____

_____

_____

Has God made you really good at something (it can be anything)? If so, what is it? Do you ever use it to help others?

_____

_____

_____

_____

_____

If you are doing these things, then thank God for working through you. If you aren't doing them, then ask God to help you!

THE HELMET OF SALVATION

THE BIG IDEA
Jesus has saved us from the kingdom of darkness, and we are free to serve Him.

SESSION AIMS
In this session, you will guide students to (1) see that the helmet of salvation is the powerful deliverance God gives us through His Son; (2) learn that salvation is something God did for us that we could never do for ourselves; and (3) understand that through this salvation we are free to serve Him with all our heart, soul, mind and strength.

THE BIGGEST VERSE
"Take the helmet of salvation" (Ephesians 6:17).

OTHER IMPORTANT VERSES
Exodus 15:2; 2 Chronicles 6:41; Psalm 74:12; Isaiah 12:2; 59:15-17; Matthew 22:35-38; Luke 3:6; Acts 4:12; Romans 1:16; 7:14,18-20; 2 Corinthians 5:17; 6:2; Colossians 1:13-14; Hebrews 9:14; 1 Peter 3:15; 1 John 4:9-10

Note: Additional options and worksheets in 8¹/₂" x 11" format for this session are available for download at **www.gospellight.com/uncommon/jh_the_armor_of_god.zip**.

STARTER

Option 1: What's in a Name? For this option, you will need an etymology dictionary or Internet access to a site that gives the origin and meaning of names.[1]

Begin the session by asking the group members if they have ever seen the play *Romeo and Juliet* by William Shakespeare. Even if they haven't seen the whole play, it's likely they are at least familiar with the balcony scene and Juliet's famous "What's in a name?" speech (act 2, scene 2, for you Bard buffs). Explain that in the play, Juliet Capulet loves a boy named Romeo whose family, the Montagues, is an archrival of her family. She complains that everything would be fine if he only had a different name—something besides "Montague."

Open a discussion by asking the students how important they think names are. Do names reflect who a person is? Begin to look up some of their names to find the meaning and origin of each one. (It's usually an eye-opener for some students who don't have any idea that their names even had a meaning beyond something that their parents call them.) Then ask the students if their name's meaning fits their personality. Do they think their lives would be any different if they had been called by another name? How much do names matter?

Explain to the group that in biblical times, names were a way of identifying a person's character and destiny. For example, *Adam* means "man," which is what he was. *Abraham* means "father of nations," which is what God called him to become. *David* means "beloved," and he is the only one in the Bible to be called a man after God's own heart. The name *Jesus* means "God is Salvation." God told Mary, His mother, this name before Jesus was born in order to boldly declare His purpose: Our God has come to save us.

Tell the group that this week they will be learning about the next piece of armor: the helmet of salvation. Equipping this helmet starts by understanding the character of the one who made salvation possible: Jesus, God our Savior.

Option 2: Cornered. For this option, you will need a room with four corners, eight pieces of paper, a marker, tape, a hat, music and a way to play it. Ahead of time, take four pieces of paper and write one number on each: 1, 2, 3, 4. Tape each numbered piece of paper to one of the four corners of your room. Next, take the other four pieces of paper and again write one number on each: 1, 2, 3, 4. Fold theses papers up and put them in your hat. Have your music ready to play.

Welcome the students to this session and ask them to gather in the center of the room. Explain that when the music starts, they are to wander around the outside of the room. When the music stops, they are to go to the closest corner and stay there.

Start the music and let it play for several seconds. Stop the music, and make sure everyone is standing at a corner. Without looking, pull a number out of the hat. Any students who are standing in the corner that has the same number as the one you selected are out of the game and must go back to the center of the room. Place the number back in the hat and start the music again. Keep going until everyone is out.

Gather the group back together. Explain that even though everyone tried his or her best not to be in one of the "out" corners, someone was always caught. In this game, there was *nowhere* to go that was always safe. In the same way, our best efforts in this life will not save us—there is nowhere for us to run. We need a Savior to rescue us from the snares of the enemy.

Conclude by stating that this is what Jesus came to earth to do. He came into our corner and defeated the enemy once and for all so that we would never again be caught "out." Because He is with always with us, we can rest safely in the salvation He provides. All we have to do is equip the next piece of armor that we will discuss today: the helmet of salvation.

MESSAGE

Option 1: Cool Dog Tricks. For this option, you will need Bibles, a volunteer who has a dog that does cool tricks, and, of course, the dog to do the tricks. (As an option, you can just find an online clip of a dog and a trainer doing tricks.)

Begin by explaining that in order to put on the helmet of salvation, we first have to understand what the word "salvation" means. In the Bible, the Hebrew and Greek words for "salvation" both have to do with the idea of deliverance— about being rescued from the power and control of someone else.[2] Bring out the trainer with his or her dog (or play the clip), and have the person show the students some awesome tricks that the dog can do. After the trainer has finished, explain to the group that the dog is under the *control* of its trainer. The dog obeys what the trainer commands because he or she has power and control over the dog's actions.

State that the Bible teaches that all humankind is born under the dominion (or control) of sin. Ask the group members what they think being "under the power" of sin means. Help them to see that it doesn't mean that we are unable to live the way God intends for us to live because we have no way to resist sin. Instead, it just means that *without God's help*, we will always act in a way that drives us away from Him rather than toward Him, because the power of sin has control over us.

Read Romans 7:14,18-20. Explain that in this passage, Paul reveals the struggle we have because we are under the dominion of sin. Even when we want to do the right thing, sometimes we end up doing the exact opposite, *because the sin in us drives us to do so.* Sin tells us to lie, and we do it. Sin tells us to cheat just this once, and we do it. Sin tells us to be jealous, and we are. We can't help it. We are like a dog who obeys its trainer. Want more proof? Think about a child—you never have to teach him or her to be bad. It comes naturally, because all humankind was placed under the dominion of sin when Adam and Eve disobeyed God.

Before everyone is so depressed they break into loud wailing and lamentation, explain that Jesus came to rescue us from the power of sin so we would be free to do the right thing, which is to serve God. Choose a volunteer to read Colossians 1:13-14. Explain to the group how this passage tells us that although we were once under the dominion of darkness and subject to its power and control, Jesus came to deliver us and save us from it. Jesus' salvation is a massive rescue that frees all of us from the power of sin.

Choose a volunteer to read Isaiah 59:15-17. Explain that this passage paints a vivid picture of our victorious, merciful Rescuer. Thousands of years ago, God's people, the nation of Israel, had been disobedient to the law of God. As a result, a neighboring enemy had conquered them. They were miserable living under the dominion of their enemy, so they called out to God for help. God saw that they would never be able to rescue themselves—they weren't strong enough—and that they would continue to stay under the power of their enemies unless He stepped in. So He did! He came and rescued His people. He drove off the enemy and delivered the nation of Israel from its oppressors.

Continue to share with the students how the New Testament offers us the same story of salvation. Because of our disobedience to God's Word, a powerful enemy has conquered us. This enemy is *sin.* We are miserable under sin's dominion but powerless to do anything about it. But when we call out to God for help, Jesus steps in to rescue us. He comes as the mighty King who, through His death and resurrection, defeated sin completely.

Connect this to the armor of God by reading Ephesians 6:14-17. Explain that the helmet is an example of salvation. The Roman soldier's helmet of Paul's time was made of either brass or bronze and was lined with felt and leather. It often had cheek and neck guards attached to it, and sometimes it also had a feather or horsehair plume at the top. The helmet protected the most vital part of the soldier: his brain. The brain not only controls unconscious activities such as breathing, but it also controls conscious functions such as reason and emotion, which help us communicate with others. By using the phrase "helmet of salvation," Paul was asserting that God's deliverance covers everything that makes up our being—our mind, our will and our emotions. Because of God's salvation, we are free from the power of sin and can now serve Him with all that we are.

Option 2: Saved! For this option, you will need Bibles, a Roman soldier's armor, pens or pencils, a volunteer and copies of the handout "Saved!" (found on the next page). Ahead of time, buy or rent a Roman soldier's armor from a costume store, or make one by using things such as a belt, a paintball vest, and so on. The main point is that you will need something to represent the belt, the breastplate, the shoes, the shield and the helmet.

Begin by reading Ephesians 6:14-17. Explain to the group that Paul used his understanding of a Roman soldier's uniform to show how God equips us to fight against the spiritual darkness of this world. Choose a volunteer to dress in the pieces of armor as you review them. End the review by drawing attention to the fact that the helmet is our example of salvation. Have your volunteer do a quick runway walk down the center of the room, and then he or she can sit back down with the group.

Explain that the Roman soldier's helmet of Paul's time, called a *galea,* was made of either brass or bronze and was lined with felt and leather. The exact design of the helmet varied over time, but generally it had cheek and neck guards and sometimes a feather or horsehair plume at the top. Ask the students what they think might be the connection between a helmet and salvation. (*The helmet protected the most vital part of the soldier: his brain.*) The brain controls not only unconscious activities such as breathing, but also conscious functions such as thoughts and emotions. By using the phrase "helmet of salvation," Paul is asserting that God's deliverance covers our mind, our will and our emotions. Because of His salvation, we are free from the power of sin and can serve Him with all of our being.

Youth Leader Tip
Sometimes students agree with the idea of salvation but haven't really experienced it. Be sure you are moving them to form a personal relationship with Christ. This means a lot of prayer and soul-searching!

Saved!

In your group, discuss these questions and then jot down your ideas.

Read Colossians 1:13-14. What kingdom were we in? What are we in now if we belong to Jesus?

_____
_____
_____
_____

Read Romans 7:14,18-20. What is the struggle explained in this verses? Is there anything from which people cannot save themselves?

_____
_____
_____
_____
_____

Read Isaiah 59:15-20. What was God appalled by? What did He do about it? What happened to the enemies? What was the response of the people who were saved?

_____
_____
_____
_____

Read Titus 3:3-7. What were we like before salvation? Why did God save us? What hope is ours now?

_____
_____
_____
_____

Divide the students into groups of 4 to 5. Pass out the handout "Saved" and pens or pencils. Have each group work through the handout. Once everyone is finished, regroup and give students an opportunity to share their responses. Make sure to stress the point that the Bible tells us that humans are born incapable of living the way God designed (sometimes referred to as "original sin"). Not everyone believes that humankind is innately sinful; in fact, in today's culture, many people (including some Christians) don't believe there is such a thing as sin. They believe that all we need to do is always make the right choices. The problem is that we cannot do this on our own.

Help the students see that if there is no sin, there is no need for a Savior. If we do not need a Savior, then we must be able to rescue ourselves though our minds, our wills and our efforts. A quick look at history reveals that even the most capable leader could not fix the problems of his or her society because the main issue existed inside of people, not outside. This problem was, and still is today, *our hearts*. Each of us is incurably selfish and bent toward evil. It is only by the power of Jesus that we can be saved from the inevitable destruction that our sinful nature will bring. The good news is that Jesus came to rescue us, and through His death and resurrection we can be saved!

DIG

Option 1: Song of Salvation. For this option, you will need Bibles. Begin by explaining to the group that the Bible speaks often of the "song of salvation." This refers to the victory song that God's people would sing when their physical enemies had been defeated. This is similar to the way fans at a ballgame go berserk when their team wins. When we consider how great is the gift of salvation that Jesus has given to us, a song should rise up in our hearts as well.

Have the students form eight groups. Hand out Bibles and assign one of the verses below to each group. Instruct them to create a song for the verse. It can be any style of music and they can add extra words to their song, but the point of the verse must come across loud and clear. Here are the verses:

- Exodus 15:2
- 2 Chronicles 6:41
- Psalm 74:12
- Isaiah 12:2

- Luke 3:6
- Acts 4:12
- Romans 1:16
- 2 Corinthians 6:2

Give each group an opportunity to present its song. (As an option, have everyone vote for his or her favorite.) When everyone is finished, choose one person from each group to read the verses straight through so that everyone can hear the actual verses on which the songs were based.

Option 2: Minds Renewed. For this option, you will need Bibles, plastic kitchen wrap, a basin, a pitcher of water and a water-soluble marker (you need one that will begin to smear when water is poured on it).

Explain to the group that the helmet is a symbol of battle. Soldiers never headed out into a fight without protecting one of their most precious organs: their brains. Likewise, we should never think we can face the spiritual darkness of this world without keeping our minds covered by the salvation we've experienced in Jesus. We must diligently re-*mind* ourselves of what He did to bring us from the kingdom of darkness into the kingdom of light.

Choose a volunteer to read Matthew 22:35-38. Ask the students to think about what it means to love God with their minds. Choose another volunteer to write the answers given by the group on a whiteboard. Then read Romans 8:5-11, and explain to the group that when we set our minds—our thoughts and desires—upon God, we can live in a way that shows our love for Him. We live out our salvation by pursuing Him in everything we do—even in what we think about.

Choose a volunteer to read Romans 12:2. Explain that before we received salvation, we were destined to become like the world around us. However, when we became Christians, we reversed direction and started to become more like Jesus. This is one of the steps in working out our salvation, and it is a transformation that happens by the renewing of our minds.

Ask the students how we can renew our minds. (*We renew our minds by reading, memorizing and thinking about what the Bible says.*) Next, hold up your hand and write the word "Jesus" across it with the water-based marker. Explain that we can know with our minds what the truth is, but unless we are diligent about guarding it, we will still be open to attack. Pour the water over your hand and into the basin. The letters should smear and start to wash off. Explain that at times we come under attack and the enemy does his best to wash away everything we thought we knew about God and salvation. The only way that we can stop this from happening is to diligently re-*mind* ourselves of the truth.

Dry your hand and rewrite the word "Jesus" on it. Begin to talk about the truths you know from the Bible, such as the fact that salvation comes from Jesus. As you speak, wrap your hand in the plastic kitchen wrap. The point is to show the students that as we think about His love, faithfulness, sacrifice and promises, we are "wrapping" our minds with the power of His Word. Filling our minds with godly thoughts in this manner will protect us against the destructive lies that the enemy tries to get us to believe.

Pour the water over your hand and into the basin. Conclude by stating that no matter what happens in our lives, if our minds are wrapped up in His promises, we are protected.

APPLY

Option 1: Put on Your Helmet. For this option, you will need time to pray.

Close today's lesson by reminding the group members that when we receive salvation through Jesus Christ, it doesn't stop there. We need to tell others God's message of deliverance so they can experience salvation as well.

Choose a volunteer to read Acts 26:16-18. Explain that these verses refer to a specific task that God gave to Paul: to take the gospel of salvation to the Gentiles. Jesus also gives us the task of sharing the good news. Choose a volunteer to read Romans 1:16 and 1 Peter 3:15. Sum up the main idea of these verses for the group: God not only wants us to receive salvation but He also wants us to be prepared to tell others about it.

Have the students quietly consider the people in their lives who have not experienced salvation through Christ. Spend time in prayer together, asking God to give each student an opportunity to tell someone else about Jesus.

Option 2: Wall Warriors 5. This is a continuation of option 2 from sessions 1–4. If you have new students, you will need more butcher paper, masking tape and markers. Ahead of time, cut the butcher paper into five-foot to six-foot pieces.

Have students continue to create their life-sized "warriors." This week, they will be drawing the helmet of salvation. Across the helmet, have students write the phrase "Jesus is salvation." Reread Ephesians 6:10-17 and Acts 4:12. Remind the students of the main idea in this week's lesson: Jesus is our salvation.

REFLECT

The following short devotions are for the students to reflect on and answer during the week. You can make a copy of these pages and distribute them to your class or download and print them from **www.gospellight.com/uncommon/jh_the_armor_of_god.zip**.

1—GRATEFUL FOR SALVATION

Jesus gave up everything to save you. When you think about what He did, you can feel special, important and grateful that He chose you. Read Romans 3:23, 6:23 and 10:9. What do these verses say about salvation?

_____

_____

_____

Read the following verses and fill in the blanks.

Psalm 136:1: "Give _____ to the LORD, for he is good, His love endures forever."

Psalm 50:23: "Those who sacrifice _____ offerings honor me, and to the blameless I will show my salvation."

Hebrews 12:28: "Therefore since we are receiving a kingdom that cannot be _____, let us be _____, and so worship God acceptably with _____ and _____."

Write a prayer thanking God for all His good gifts. Spend some time specifically thanking Him for the wonderful gift of salvation.

_____

_____

_____

2—DEBT CANCELLED!

When you face hard times in your life, don't forget that the helmet of salvation is always covering your mind. Keep your thoughts on Jesus, because He loves you and gave up everything to save you. Read Matthew 18:23-27. In these verses, Jesus tells a story. In your own words, write down what happened.

_____

_____

_____

This story should teach us to forgive others, but it should also help us see how great God is. In this story, a servant owed his master 10,000 talents. It would have taken him 15 years to earn one talent. He could never have repaid it in a lifetime! The master had the right to sell the man and his children as slaves to pay the debt. However, the master chose to forgive the servant and cancel the debt. The servant did not have to pay what he owed.

We also have a huge debt—a debt of sin. We owe God more than we could ever repay. We have sinned in so many ways that the only way we could be right with God would be for Him to cancel our debt. Thankfully, that is exactly what Jesus did when He died on the cross for us! Just like the man in the story, we have so much to be thankful for!

Say a prayer thanking God for canceling your debt of sin. Thank Him for the price He paid for your great debt.

3—WASHED FROM SIN

God made a way for your sins to be washed away. That way of cleansing is salvation, and it is free! Describe the way you looked, felt and smelled the last time you got really dirty after playing sports or being out in the rain and mud.

_____

_____

_____

Describe how you looked, felt and smelled after you took a shower and got clean.

_____

_____

_____

_____

Each of us is spiritually dirty because of sin. The only way we can get spiritually clean is if we ask Jesus for it. Jesus will respond by washing us until we are spotless. Look up Hebrews 9:14. What does this verse say about how Jesus washes you clean from sin?

_____

_____

_____

Now look up 1 John 1:7. What does this verse say about how Jesus cleanses us from sin?

_____

_____

_____

Say a prayer, thanking Jesus for washing your sins away and making you clean.

4—NEW LIFE

Sometimes it is hard to understand that when we receive salvation from God, we also receive new life. Look up the following verses and write down what the Bible says about this new life:

2 Corinthians 5:17: "Therefore, if anyone is in Christ, he is a ____ _____; the ___ has gone, the ____ has come!"

Colossians 3:9-10: "Do not lie to each other, since you have taken off your ____ self with its practices and have put on the _____ self, which is being _____ in _____ in the image of its Creator."

When Christ died to save you, He saved you from the way you used to live—a way that would ultimately lead to your spiritual death. Jesus has made you into a new creation! You are now a son or daughter of God. Think about how wonderful this is for a moment. How have you changed since you accepted Christ? How are you still changing?

_____

_____

_____

Today, thank God for giving you salvation and making you a new creation.

THE COVERING
OF PRAYER

THE BIG IDEA

The Word of God, spoken in prayer through the Holy Spirit, brings us freedom and victory.

SESSION AIMS

In this session, you will guide students to (1) see that the armor of God begins and ends with reliance on Him; (2) understand that the last piece of the defensive armor is Spirit-led prayer; and (3) comprehend that through this kind of prayer, we defeat darkness and advance God's kingdom.

THE BIGGEST VERSE

"Pray in the Spirit on all occasions with all kinds of prayers and requests. With this in mind, be alert and always keep on praying for the saints" (Ephesians 6:18).

OTHER IMPORTANT VERSES

Deuteronomy 31:6; Daniel 10:12-14; Jonah 3:4-10; Matthew 6:5-8; Luke 11:2-4; 18:1-8; Romans 8:26-27; 15:30-31; 2 Corinthians 1:10-11; Ephesians 1:17-21; Colossians 4:2-4,12; Hebrews 4:12; 1 John 5:14-15

Note: Additional options and worksheets in 8¹/₂" x 11" format for this session are available for download at **www.gospellight.com/uncommon/jh_the_armor_of_god.zip**.

STARTER

Option 1: Armor Ads. For this option, you will need some creative students and one set of Roman armor (whatever visual aids you have been using each week is fine—plain leather belts, paintball vests, or whatever).

Welcome students and have them form into five groups. State that in order to be sure that they have not forgotten the significance of each piece of armor, you are going to have each group come up with a 30- to 60-second commercial for *one* piece of the armor (the belt of truth, the breastplate of righteousness, the shield of faith, the shoes of the gospel of peace, and the helmet of salvation). Give students a few minutes to prepare, and make sure that everyone in every group is involved in some way. Then have each group present their ad. Be ready to fill in the gaps as needed so that this is not only a comic routine by some of the finest junior stand-ups in the country but also a valuable recap of what you have labored to teach the past five weeks.

Once every group has shown their ad, explain that this session will focus on the "covering of prayer," which is specifically praying in the Spirit. Prayer is a powerful tool in the Christian's arsenal. When we put it on with the other pieces of armor—effectively covering ourselves with it—we will find it is a powerful tool that can drive the darkness out and help us see God's kingdom on earth![1]

Option 2: How Many Times? For this option, you will need a brick of cheese, a cutting board, crackers and a sharp knife.

Hold up the brick of cheese. Ask for students to guess how many times you can cut the brick in half until it is too small to cut any further. Cut the brick in half. Then cut a half in half. Keep going until you cannot cut anymore. At that point explain that perhaps if you had a knife with a finer blade, you could go even further, but this is as good as it gets here. (*Note:* From a purely philosophical perspective, you can cut anything in half because there is an infinite amount of space between points. That means that no matter how small, you always have room to cut it in half again. It's called Zeno's paradox. But that's another lesson.)

<u>Youth Leader Tip</u>
If you are a person with a passion for prayer, that will infect your ministry. Share with your group the impact that prayer and worship has made on your life and how it has benefited you.[2]

Make up some cheese and crackers for your group members. As you do, explain that during this session on the armor of God, we will be discussing the "covering of prayer." Prayer is a powerful piece of equipment in our arsenal, and we need to take advantage of it. When we do, we will find that prayer is a powerful tool to drive out the darkness and see God's kingdom advance!

MESSAGE

Option 1: Conformed by Prayer. For this option, you will need one small inexpensive journal or composition book per student, pens or pencils, play dough and a play dough mold. Ahead of time, write *one* of the following questions on the first page of each journal. You will end up with a set of eight journals, all of which have a different question on the first page. Make as many sets as you need for the number of students you serve.

- When was a time in your life when you had a prayer that was miraculously answered?
- Should everyone pray? Why or why not?
- What is prayer? What is prayer *not*?
- What happens when two people pray for opposite outcomes of the same situation?
- Does God hear everyone's prayers, including those from people of other religions? How do you know?
- Do you think God appreciates some prayers better than others? Why or why not?
- Where is the best place to pray? Why is it the best?
- Where is the worst place to pray? Why is it the worst?

Divide the group members into small groups of six to eight people. Hand each student one journal and a pen. Explain that they will have two minutes to read and respond to the prompt on the front page of the journal. When you call "time," each student will pass his journal to the student sitting on his left, and you will continue in this manner until the journals have made it through the group.

When your group is finished with this exercise, ask the students to share something they found intriguing in the responses they read or wrote. There will most likely be a few points that shine like a beacon—and there will probably be some laconic one-word responses such as "yes." Explain that there are lots of things we could say about prayer, but the most important point is that prayer provides us with a connection with God. When we pray, seek God's will for our lives and do what He says, He will begin to "conform" us. This conforming is a lot of what we've been talking about during the past several weeks—the armor of God is all about us being fitted with the likeness of our Father and being made into His image so that we live lives that reflect His truth and peace.

To illustrate the idea of conforming, invite a volunteer up and give him or her a can of play dough and a play dough mold. Have the volunteer shape the dough and then pop it out of the mold so everyone can see it. Explain that when we spend time in prayer, God's Spirit conforms us into His image so we become more and more shaped into the person He desires us to be. How does this happen? When we pray, we surrender to Him. As we surrender, His power changes us.

Read Ephesians 6:17-18. Explain that the sword of the Spirit refers to God's Word spoken over our circumstances as the Holy Spirit leads (see Matthew 4:4, 7,10). If we are to take our stand against the spiritual darkness of this world, we must be always ready to take up the Word of God and in prayer declare what He has said to be the truth. One important way we hold out this powerful Word of God is by praying in the Spirit. Praying in the Spirit can have several different meanings. It can mean "by means of," "with the help of," "in the sphere of" and "in connection to." Praying in the Spirit does not refer to the words we are saying; instead, it refers to *how* we are praying—or *in whose strength*.

Conclude by stating that it is no accident that the armor of God begins with a command to be strong in the Lord and ends with a command to take up His Word and pray. We live in a dark world that is devoid of truth and doomed to destruction—and there is nothing we could do about it in and of ourselves. But God, who loves us, broke through the darkness so we could experience freedom and victory. Have a volunteer read Romans 8:26. Explain that praying in the Spirit is praying with the help of the Spirit and living in such a way that we are always attuned to what God is saying to us. Spirit-led prayer can enable us to clearly see the truth and, knowing that we have victory, confidently declare it to the world around us.

Option 2: Power of Spirit-filled Prayer. For this option, you need Bibles and three or four volunteers who can share about a time when prayer changed the outcome of a specific circumstance in their lives. (This is a great way to get pastors and other church leaders to spend a few minutes with the youth for some old-school face time!)

Welcome students and read Ephesians 6:18. Explain that during the past few weeks, we have been discussing the armor of God. "Praying in the Spirit" is part of our weaponry against the enemy, but it is a bit different. In fact, from the way in which this passage in Ephesians was written, we can understand that Paul intends for us to put on each piece of equipment *with prayer.* In other words, as we protect ourselves with God's truth, righteousness, peace, faith and salvation, prayer should cover everything we do. Then we are to continue on and pray as God guides us "on all occasions with all kinds of prayers and requests."

Invite your volunteers to share with the group how prayer brought victory in their lives. If appropriate, let the students ask questions. When the volunteers are finished, have the volunteers read aloud these verses about prayer:

- Luke 18:1-8: We should be persistent in prayer.
- Colossians 4:2-4: We should devote ourselves to prayer. (Prayer is not just a once-in-a-while kind of activity.)
- Matthew 6:5-8: We should be humble when we pray.
- Romans 8:26-27: The Holy Spirit should lead our prayers.

Explain that we live in a world devoid of truth and doomed to destruction, and there is nothing we can do about it in and of ourselves. But God, who loves us, broke through the darkness and brought us His Word and His Holy Spirit, our helper, so we could experience freedom and victory. Praying in the Spirit means praying with the aid of the Spirit, allowing Him to lead, empower and teach us. Prayer should cover everything we do. It allows us to see the truth and, knowing that we have victory, confidently declare it to the world around us.

DIG

Option 1: Prayer Warriors. For this option, you will need Bibles, copies of "Prayer Warriors" (found on the next page), and pens or pencils.

Explain that the Bible gives us many examples of men and women who prayed and then witnessed the power of God act in their present situation. Have students form groups of three to four. Give each group a Bible, a copy of "Prayer Warriors" and a pen or pencil. Instruct them to work through the passages together and then gather back together to share responses.

If you have a lot of lively students, you may want to have them reenact one of the stories for everyone's general edification and enjoyment, but just talking is fine as well. However you have your students share, be sure to have them

PRAYER WARRIORS

Look up each of the following passages and read about some of the people in the Bible whose prayers changed lives. Write down some things that stand out to you and note how prayer was used in each story to display God's awesome power.

PRAYER WARRIOR: ELIJAH

Story: 1 Kings 17:1; 18:1,19-46

Set-up: Ahab, the king of Israel, and his wife, Jezebel, had abandoned the Lord and encouraged idol worship throughout the nation. Because of this overt rebellion, God had not allowed it to rain for three years. The Lord sent Elijah, a prophet, to set things right.

PRAYER WARRIOR: DANIEL

Story: Daniel 2:1-49

Set-up: Daniel and his friends had been taken as captives when Babylon conquered Jerusalem. They were living as servants of the Babylonian king, but they were committed to keeping their hearts devoted to God no matter what.

PRAYER WARRIORS: PAUL AND SILAS

Story: Acts 16:16-40

Set-up: Paul and Silas had cast a demon out of a girl and, as a result, she no longer had the power to predict the future. Her owners became angry that they had lost their source of income and had Paul and Silas thrown into jail.

consider in each passage how prayer was an important tool that God used to display His power and establish His kingdom. End by reminding students that prayer is a powerful part of our spiritual equipment, and that when we pray, God will bring His power into our lives.

Option 2: Prayer Questions. For this option, you will need Bibles and talkative students. Use the following questions to generate a conversation about prayer. If your group is too large to effectively discuss these questions, arrange for youth leaders to lead a discussion with smaller groups. Ideally, it's best to have about 8 to 12 students per group.

1. *If God is all-powerful, why does He want us to pray?* Explain that God is all-powerful, but He chose to set things up as a partnership. We join with God as He does His work in the world, and this is especially true in prayer. Have a volunteer read Romans 15:30-31, 2 Corinthians 1:10-11 and Colossians 4:12. Ask students to comment on these verses, which tell us that when we pray, God resolves struggles and advances the gospel. This seems to imply that when we don't pray, things don't work well. So, prayer is a crucial part of seeing God's kingdom advance. That's one reason to pray.

2. *Does God's will change because of our prayers?* Explain that when we pray, we are *not* talking God into doing something or changing His will. However, there are times in the Bible when prayer changed the actions of people, which in turn caused God to change His plans on something. Have a volunteer read Jonah 3:4-10. State that while God did not bring destruction on Nineveh, His will and His heart never changed in this situation.

3. *What are we to ask for when we pray?* Have a volunteer read 1 John 5:14-15. State that when we pray, we are to ask for things that are in agreement with God's will as revealed in the Bible. We can know what these are by getting into His Word. An example of this can be found in Ephesians 1:17-21. Have a volunteer read this aloud, and then discuss what this passage tells us about how we are to pray.

4. *Is there a specific way to pray or some kind of model for prayer?* Explain that Jesus gave His disciples a model for prayer, which is often

called "The Lord's Prayer." Have a volunteer read Luke 11:2-4. State
that Jesus did not give this prayer to His disciples to have them recite it verbatim but just to give them a general structure for prayer.
The prayer begins with acknowledging our *relationship* with God:
He is our Father. Then we *worship* Him and allow our minds and
hearts to recall how great and awesome He truly is. Next, we pray
that *His kingdom*—His rule and reign—will continue to be estab-
lished here on earth. We are to ask for *provision*, so that we have
what we need, and *forgiveness*, both for ourselves and others. We
end by asking for His *guidance* to lead us away from temptation.

5. *What if our prayers aren't answered?* The Bible gives us specific reasons why prayers go unanswered, and most of them are negative—
   something of which we must confess and repent. Sometimes it is
   the result of sin (see 1 Peter 3:12), or because we ask for selfish reasons (see James 4:3), or because we are living in ways that displease
   God (see 1 John 3:22). If we are holding a grudge against someone, that can hinder our prayers as well (see Matthew 6:14-15). On
   the other hand, sometimes prayers go unanswered even though
   we are doing everything right. Have a volunteer read Daniel 10:12-
   14. Explain that in this case, the angel was hindered in delivering
   God's response to Daniel's prayer for understanding. This is one
   reason why Jesus tells us to "pray and not give up" in Luke 18:1.

6. *What if we don't feel anything after we pray?* Prayer is an act of faith,
   so what we feel or don't feel really doesn't matter all that much. It
   is what we *do* that counts. If we commit to being persistent and
   consistent in praying, God will work in our hearts and we will grow
   to sense more and more that our prayers are full of His power.

APPLY

Option 1: Enlist in the Service. For this option, you will need a Bible and a pen.
Ahead of time, write the title "In His Service" at the top of one of the blank
pages in the back of the Bible.

Begin by stating that you want to give students an opportunity to openly
express their decision to "enlist in the service" of the King. Pass around the
Bible and a pen and ask those who want to do so to sign their names as a way

of declaring their intention to "enlist" as a follower of Jesus (by the way, your name should be at the top of the list!). Students can pen their John Hancock anywhere on the page. Explain that signing their name isn't magical and doesn't make them a better Christian; it is only a symbol of what their hearts have already committed to do.

Wrap everything up by reminding the group that as we have talked about the nature of God—His truth, righteousness, peace and faith—we have learned that in Him we have all we need to face the challenges ahead and bring glory to His name. Spend some time praying for your students by name, asking God to continue to work in their lives and draw their hearts closer and closer to Him. End by reading Ephesians 6:10-18. Let them know that you will keep praying for them personally.

Option 2: Wall Warriors 6. This is the conclusion of option 2 from sessions 1–5. If you have new students, you will need more butcher paper, masking tape and markers. Ahead of time, cut the butcher paper into 5- to 6-foot pieces.

This week, the group members will be adding pieces of equipment to their wall warriors to close out this activity. First, to remind them that prayer is to be equipped with the armor of God, have them write the word "prayer" on each individual piece. Next, explain that during the next several weeks, you are going to be talking about the one offensive weapon that God has given us: the Sword of the Spirit, which is the Word of God. Have them draw a sword either in their warrior's hand or in the belt of truth (a soldier would tuck away his sword in his belt when not in use). Down the blade of the sword, have students write "The Word of God." Read Ephesians 6:17-18 and Hebrews 4:12.

Because this is the final session in which students will be adding equipment to their wall warriors, they can take them home at this point as a way to recall the lessons they have learned. The wall warrior can also serve to remind them to equip the armor of God each day by living lives that reflect the nature and love of the heavenly Father.

Youth Leader Tip

Students should feel free to be honest about their thoughts and doubts without fear of being condemned. Encourage this by letting kids who voice "unChristian" comments know that you aren't offended, but that you will seek to find an answer with them.

REFLECT

The following short devotions are for the students to reflect on and answer during the week. You can make a copy of these pages and distribute them to your class or download and print them from **www.gospellight.com/uncommon/jh_the_armor_of_god.zip**.

1—PRAYING FOR OUR NEEDS

Prayer is an important part of your spiritual armor. When you talk with God, your commander, you can receive help and strength to resist the attacks of the enemy. When you take your needs to God, you can be confident that He will give you what we need to fight the battle. Read Philippians 4:6. According to this verse, how are you to present your requests to God?

- ❑   With understanding
- ❑   With anxiety
- ❑   Calmly and humbly
- ❑   With thanksgiving

Read Matthew 10:29-31. What does this passage tell you about how God cares about everything you are going through?

_____

_____

_____

What does this passage tell you about your worth to God?

_____

_____

_____

Write down one thing that you need God to do in your life right now.

_____

_____

_____

2—PRAYING FOR OTHERS

You are not alone in this spiritual battle—there are many others around you who need help as well. Prayer is one way you can help support others. Read

James 5:13-14 and fill in the blanks below to find out some of the times when you should pray:

> Is any one of you in _____? He should _____. Is anyone _____? Let him sing _____ of _____. Is any one of you _____? He should call the elders of the church to _____ over him and anoint him with oil in the name of the Lord.

Now read James 5:15. What does this verse say will happen when you pray for someone?

_____

_____

_____

What do you think "the prayer offered in faith" means?

_____

_____

_____

Think of someone you know who is going through a tough time or just needs some encouragement. Write a prayer asking God to help that person.

_____

_____

_____

3—PRAYING THE WORD

In every battle, there comes a point where you will not know what to do next—or even what to pray. What do you do then? One thing you can do is claim the promises that God has given to you in the Bible. Look up the following Scriptures and write down what they say God will do when you need His strength:

Psalm 44:6-7: _____

_____

Luke 10:19: _____

_____

John 16:33: _____

_____

2 Timothy 4:18: _____

_____

How can you remember these promises when you face times when everything seems to be going wrong?

_____

_____

_____

4—PRAYERS OF PRAISE

When you put on the full armor of God, you will be able to resist the attacks of
the enemy and win the battle. You will win! So, what do you do then? A good
idea is to say a prayer of thanks to God for giving you the victory. Read 1 Chronicles 16:8. What does this verse say we should do?

- ❑   Call on God's name
- ❑   Give thanks to God
- ❑   Tell everyone what He has done
- ❑   All of the above

Read 1 Thessalonians 5:18. In what situations are we to thank God? Why?

_____

_____

_____

Think of one victory you have had recently and write it below.

_____

_____

_____

_____

Remember that prayer is an important part of your spiritual armor. It is a way
you can receive guidance and strength from God to help you throughout
your day. So make prayer a part of your daily life!

SUIT UP!

Wearing protective armor is just as important for soldiers today as it was back in the apostle Paul's day. Of course, the protective gear has changed a bit over the years. Today's armor is lighter and built to withstand gunfire rather than sword attacks. Yet the purpose is the same: to protect the soldier's life.

Modern soldiers wear a *ballistic vest* typically made of Kevlar, a high-strength flexible material that can resist bullets. Sometimes, metal or ceramic plates are inserted into the vests to provide additional protection from rifle shots (and even knife attacks). A ballistic vest can help a soldier survive not only gunfire but also shrapnel from explosions and fragments from hand grenades.

As in Roman times, the modern soldier's *belt* is used for storing weapons, but today it is also used for storing ammo and other items needed for combat on the field. Soldiers wear *combat helmets* and often a ballistic facemask for protection from flying bullets or shrapnel. Some military helmets are also designed to reduce damage from concussions caused by explosions.

Modern soldiers wear *combat boots* that are specially designed to give their feet protection and footing in different terrains. The current boots are tan, "rough-out" (non-shiny), and are made of leather, nylon and synthetic leather. The boots protect not only the soldier's feet but also his or her ankles, and come in waterproof, hot weather and rough terrain versions.

Shields are typically used by soldiers, SWAT teams or police officers as a part of the company's riot gear. Most are made of a clear polycarbonate that protects the user from shrapnel, thrown projectiles and "splash" from weapons such as Molotov cocktails. (They are also good for pushing back unruly crowds.)

So, how effective is all this high-tech body armor? Well, in October 2006, Gunnery Sergeant Shawn Dempsey was helping a small girl cross a street in Iraq when a sniper shot him in the back. The bullet left a one-inch hole in his armor, but he survived with just a painful bruise. "I can tell you it's effective," he said.[1]

Another marine, Lance Corporal Edward Knuth, was hit while his squad was searching a market beside a main road. The force of the bullet, which Knuth reported was "like a smacking sound," knocked him to his knees. It left a coin-sized hole in the metal plate in his armor.[2]

Just as in Roman times, the effectiveness of armor is often determined by whether or not the soldier is actually wearing it. Armor, both then and now, is bulky, hot and often makes it difficult for the soldier to maneuver. However, when worn properly, it can save his or her life. In the same way, the armor of God won't protect us unless we make the choice to put it on each day.

So, suit up!

UNIT II

The Offensive Weapon

I'm glad we don't have to don the armor of God and dive into Scripture by ourselves. Like most things in life, God has designed us to live in community in the way we stand against darkness.

When I think about community, I think about a story I once heard about the famous twentieth century pastor and evangelist D. L. Moody. Word had reached Moody that a member of his church had decided to stop attending worship services. More than that, this church member had chosen to sever all relationships with other believers.

Both curious and disturbed, Moody decided to visit this man at his home. It was a cold winter day, so the two men sat bundled in the living room with a fire burning in a fireplace nearby. The congregation member explained to his pastor that the reason he had decided to stop attending church and fellowshipping with other believers was that he didn't need to have relationships with others in order to follow Jesus. In response, Pastor Moody gave reason after reason why it was good both to go to church and to have relationships with other followers of Christ. The church member deftly refuted each one.

Finally, Moody chose a different strategy. In total silence, Moody walked toward the fireplace and used tongs to remove one of the glowing coals from the fire. Then he placed it on the brick floor, several inches from the fire. Soon, the orange glow of the coal got a little darker and a bit more gray. Moody and the congregation member watched as the warmth of the coal was totally lost and the coal turned completely dark.

The man turned to Moody and said, "Pastor Moody, I get your point. I will see you in church next week."

In all facets of our relationship with God, when we lose contact with other believers, we lose passion. We lose fervor. We lose our fire. When it comes to the powerful weapon of Scripture, we don't need to dive into it and then live out its insights on our own. The church—our fellow brothers and sisters in Christ—can stand with us, study Scripture alongside us, and support us through their prayers and encouragement.

In my own life, I have found it much easier to lean into the powerful Word of God that is explored in the next six lessons when I ask my friends and family to step into battle with me. I am at my best when I am strengthened by a trustworthy and supportive community.

I'm guessing you are too.

Kara Powell
Executive Director of the Fuller Youth Institute
Assistant Professor of Youth, Family and Culture
Fuller Theological Seminary

THE BIBLE IS UNIQUE

BIG IDEA

The Bible, the only offensive weapon in our spiritual arsenal, is a unique revelation of the true and living God.

SESSION AIMS

In this session, you will guide students to (1) realize the uniqueness of the Bible as God's specific revelation of Himself to us; (2) accept the authority of Scripture and appreciate its benefits; and (3) run in hot pursuit of our awesome Lord through a deeper understanding of the Bible.

BIGGEST VERSE

"Open my eyes that I may see wonderful things in your law" (Psalm 119:18).

OTHER IMPORTANT VERSES

Psalm 119:25-32,103,105; Proverbs 2:1-5; Isaiah 46:10; 53; Jeremiah 23:29; Daniel 10–11; Micah 5:2; Matthew 4:4; John 1:14; 17:3; 20:31; Romans 1:20; Ephesians 1:17; 5:25-26; 6:17; 2 Timothy 3:16; Hebrews 1:1-3; James 1:23-25; 1 Peter 1:23; 2:2

Note: Additional options and worksheets in 8^1/$_2$" x 11" format for this session are available for download at **www.gospellight.com/uncommon/jh_the_armor_of_god.zip**.

STARTER

Option 1: Word Fishing. For this option, you will need your Bible, a whiteboard, a dry erase marker, a cat (preferably live, but a stuffed one will work), a plastic pool (about four feet in diameter), water, several sets of blocks with letters on the sides (available in the toddler section of most toy stores—or maybe in your church nursery), a prize, four small fish nets and a plastic tarp. Ahead of time, place the tarp under the pool and fill it with water, and put the blocks in the water.

Begin by stating that for the past several weeks we have focused on the defensive armor that Paul lists in Ephesians 6:14-18. For the next six weeks, we will be turning our attention to one weapon in our arsenal: the sword of the Spirit, which is the Bible. Given the fact that this is the only weapon that we have been given, it is important for us to really seek to understand this complex and often-misunderstood weapon of spiritual warfare. For this reason, this new series will answer all their questions about the Bible. (Just kidding!) Actually, what we hope to discover in these next six sessions are the following:

1. Why we believe the Bible is the authentic and inspired Word of God
2. What the Bible has to say about who God is
3. What the Bible says that God desires from us, His followers

Explain that words are a miracle. When the students question this, state that the fact that we can take lines and squiggles (write the letters *t*, *a* and *c* on the whiteboard), attach a sound to them (point back to the letters and say each sound individually), put them in a certain order (write the word *cat*), and then communicate an idea from our brains to someone else is simply amazing (bring out the cat)! The funny lines on the whiteboard represent the cat that you are now holding.

Explain that other countries use different lines and sounds, but the process is the same. Write *el gato* (Spanish) and *le chat* (French) on the board. State that words represent ideas and thoughts that someone is trying to communicate. To illustrate this, the group members are going to see what ideas they can communicate to each other by doing a quick fishing relay.

Divide the students into four teams and give each a fishing net. Explain that at your signal, one person from each team is to run to the pool and fish out a block. That person will take the block back to his or her team and hand the net to another student, who will then run back to fish out another block. As a team, they are to write as many words with their growing list of letters as possible—

any blocks not used will be deducted from their score. If you're feeling merciful, you can tell the groups that blocks can be used to form more than one word. If you're not so merciful, explain that each block can only be used once.

After five minutes, signal the teams to stop fishing and writing. Award 100 points for each letter in a completed and correctly spelled word. If you gave the teams the option of using letters in more than one word, you will need to have them move the blocks to the different words as you calculate. Deduct 100 points for each unused block. Award a bonus of 500 points for the longest word. Give the winning team a prize.

Conclude by stating that God can speak to us through the many words He has written about Himself. We call God's written words the Bible. He has given us the Bible so that He can communicate to us what He is like and what He wants for our lives. And, as Paul states in Ephesians, we are to use this weapon to push back the darkness and win battles against our enemy. Hold up your Bible, and tell the group that today they are going to look at this big, black Book and see why it's so unique and so important to their lives.

Option 2: Word Relay. For this option, you will need your Bible, two whiteboards, dry erase markers and candy or other prizes. Ahead of time, write "word" on each of the whiteboards and set them up at the front of the room for a relay game. Angle the boards away from each other so that only one team can see each board. Place a dry erase marker at the foot of each board.

Greet the group members and ask if the group members can list each of the pieces of the armor of God that you have studied so far. (*The belt of truth, the breastplate of righteousness, the shoes of the gospel of peace, the shield of faith, the helmet of salvation, and the covering of prayer.*) State that today, we will shift our attention to the sword of the Spirit, which is the Bible. This is the only weapon listed in Ephesians 6:14-18, so it is important for us to understand how to use it. For this reason, during the next few weeks we will be exploring why the Bible is unique, how we can know it is true, what is the main message of the Bible, and how we can use it in our daily lives.

Divide the group members into two teams. Have team #1 sit facing one whiteboard and team #2 sit facing the other whiteboard. Explain that at your signal, one person from each team will race to the whiteboard, pick up the marker and create a new word by changing only one letter of the original word "word." As an example, go to one of the boards and replace the "d" with a "k," changing "word" to "work." Explain that the next person to come up will now have to change one letter from "work" and create a new word, perhaps "fork."

Instruct the teams to write each new word underneath the original so that they can see how the word is being transformed. The object of the game is to see how many new words each team can create. You can point out that though only one team member can run to the board to write the new word, the whole team can brainstorm words as a group.

After five minutes, signal a stop and review the words each team created, awarding 100 points for each new word. (You can add bonus points for creativity if you want.) Give candy or other prizes to the winning team.

Transition by stating that it is amazing these lines and squiggles called letters can represent things and ideas. Just think—these letters, when combined in the right order, can communicate ideas from our brains to other people, revealing what we're thinking. Words are really a gift from God, and He has given us a special Word to reveal to us what He is like and what He wants for us as His followers. As we now know, this is the Bible, and it represents the weapon in our spiritual arsenal. However, for it to be any good to us as a weapon, we have to understand it and know how to use it. For this reason, today we're going to look at what makes the Bible such a unique and important book.

MESSAGE

Option 1: Lost in a Fog. For this option you will need your Bible, a fog machine (you can rent these from most party supply stores), index cards, a pen and masking tape. Ahead of time, use the index cards to make two sets of identically numbered cards (1, 2, 3, 4). You will need one card for each student in attendance. In addition, practice using the fog machine and the fan so you know how much time it takes to fill your meeting room and how long it takes to clear it away.

Hold up your Bible and state that the Word of God is *the* way God has given us to begin to understand specifically who He is and what He is like. Only God can give us a way to know Him, and only He can reveal Himself to us. If we didn't have the Bible, we would be clueless as to His nature and His ways. We would be searching for something we could never clearly see.

Youth Leader Tip

In this session, we are establishing the uniqueness of the Bible and why we can trust it. Students will inevitably be asking questions that deal with future topics. This is good! Encourage them to keep coming back for more in-depth discussions.

Turn on the fog machine. Explain that without the Word of God, this is how we live our lives. We can't see Him clearly, and we are lost. As the fog begins to fill up your room, divide students into two even-numbered groups and have them sit down in lines. For each group, tape a number card from one set of cards to each person's back (make sure the person can't see his or her number). Also, make sure the numbers are not in order as you tape them. Each line should end up using the same set of numbers—which is the reason why you needed even lines.

At your signal, the group members are to *carefully* crawl around the room (no standing, kneeling, getting on furniture, and so forth) looking for the person from the other line who has the same number taped to his or her back. They are not allowed to yell their number out but only share their numbers with individual students they encounter while crawling. When the pairs find each other, they are to crawl to the side of the room, clearing more space for those still searching. When everyone has found his or her partner, turn off the fog machine. Have the students stay where they are until you have finished this option. The fog will disappear fairly quickly, which will help bring home your point.

Explain that the group members needed help when there was fog in the room in order to find the other person. The same thing holds true when we talk about knowing God. Without His help and His specific revelation, we can never really know Him.[1] In a general way, we know God through what He has created. Read Romans 1:20 and explain that in this passage, Paul says that creation points to God's attributes and power. The complexity and harmony of nature show that someone greater *must* exist.

Sum up the message by revealing to the students that God saw our need to have a specific way of knowing Him and to find out who He was and what He wanted for His people. He knew we needed something more than what He had created. So He gave us His Word, the Bible. By now the fog should have settled. Hold up your Bible and explain that the Bible clears away the fog and gives us the ability to begin to really know God.

Option 2: What's in the Box? For this option, you will need your Bible, a shoebox with a lid, an orange (or another object), wrapping paper, transparent tape and tissue paper. Ahead of time, use the wrapping paper to wrap the box and the lid *separately*. Wrap the orange in the tissue paper and place it and your Bible in the box.

Begin by holding up the box. Ask the students what they would do to figure out what was inside this if they couldn't open it. Would they smell it? That probably wouldn't give them many clues about what it actually was unless it was something that was very fragrant (like a rose). What if they shook it? They might hear a familiar sound and make a good guess about what's inside, but it wouldn't be completely accurate. An X-ray would give them a better idea—they might be able to tell the object's basic form and shape. However, they wouldn't have the full picture of what it was. They wouldn't know its color or full dimensions. They might even misread the X-ray and get it completely wrong.

As you're talking, pass the box around and give students a chance to guess what's inside. (Remind them not to be destructive.) There may be a few students who guess correctly, which is okay. This actually enhances the point, because even if they guess correctly, they can't verify the accuracy of their guess without opening the box. There will always be the chance that they are wrong.

Once they have made their guesses, continue by asking the group members what they think is the only way to really know what is inside the box. The answer is to take the lid off. What if they can't take off the lid? Then they can never really know what is inside. Transition by asking the group to think about the concept of knowing God. All knowledge about Him is unknowable apart from Him. In other words, we can't know God unless He reveals Himself to us. Hold up the box and state this is much like a closed box we cannot open. The knowledge of what's inside is forever hidden from us if it were never opened.

Explain that when we look at our world, we can instinctively know that something greater than ourselves must exist. The order and perfection of the world around us is too amazing to deny that fact. Hold up the box and shake it. Explain that by shaking the box, we can get a general idea what is in there, and in the same way, we can get an idea of what God is like by looking at the world He created. However, it's only a general idea. Read Romans 1:20 and explain that nature doesn't give us a complete picture of who God actually is. It points to God's attributes and power, but it doesn't tell us anything about His plan for the world. We need something more.

Bring home the point by asking the students what they think is the only way to really know what God is like. (*He must reveal Himself to us; He must take the lid off of the box.*) Now ask specifically how He has done this. In other words, how did He take the lid off the box? (*Through His Word, the Bible.*)

Take the lid off of the box and pull out the orange or other object. Congratulate anyone who managed to guess correctly. Then explain that God has given us a way of understanding who He is and what He wants for His people. The Bible is a written revelation of God to us—His very words. By looking at the Bible, we can understand God's character, attributes and plan for our lives.

Conclude by asking students if they think the Bible tells us everything there is to know about God. The answer is that it *doesn't* tell us everything—there is no way to know everything about God here on earth. However, the Bible does tell us everything we *need* to know. God has revealed Himself to us through His Word because He loves us and wants to have a close, intimate relationship with us. He wants us to know Him and to understand how precious we are to Him. This is why the Bible is a unique and priceless gift.

DIG

Option 1: The Bible Is Like a . . . For this option, you will need several Bibles, a mirror, a sword, a seed, a bottle of water, a flashlight, a lighter, a hammer, milk, bread, honey, tables, a copy of "The Bible Is Like a . . ." (found on the next page) and pens or pencils. Ahead of time, place the items on tables set up along the perimeter of your meeting room. (One or two items per table tends to work best if you have the space.)

Begin this option by asking the group the following questions:

- What does the word "holy" mean? (*Set apart for a special use.*)
- Why is the word "holy" on the cover of most Bibles—why is God's Word called the "Holy" Bible? (*The Bible is a unique revelation of God that is set apart from all other books.*)
- Why is the Bible so holy? (*Because it is the Word of God, His revelation of Himself to us.*)

Continue by stating that today you want the group members to begin to appreciate the Bible's holiness—its set-apartness—by delving into some of the ways the Bible brings God's blessing to their lives. They are going to go on a Bible-verse spree. This is somewhat like a shopping spree, but the only thing that it will cost them is a little bit of time.

Divide the students into groups of three and give each group a Bible, a copy of "The Bible Is Like a . . ." and a pen or pencil. Direct the groups' attention to all of the items placed on the tables around the room. They are to spread out among the tables and match each verse on their copy of "The Bible Is Like a . . ." handout with the right item. They should write in the answer on their handouts, and after this they need to get together with their group and try to figure out the reason why that item would be used as a metaphor for the Bible.

THE BIBLE IS LIKE A . . .

Locate the item that corresponds to each verse listed below, and then give one reason why you chose that item.

Read **JAMES 1:23-25**. What item did you choose? _____
How is this item like the Bible? _____

Read **HEBREWS 4:12**. What item did you choose? _____
How is this item like the Bible? _____

Read **1 PETER 1:23**. What item did you choose? _____
How is this item like the Bible? _____

Read **EPHESIANS 5:25-26**. What item did you choose? _____
How is this item like the Bible? _____

Read **PSALM 119:105**. What item did you choose? _____
How is this item like the Bible? _____

Read **JEREMIAH 23:29**. What items did you choose? _____
How are these items like the Bible? _____

Read **1 PETER 2:2**. What item did you choose? _____
How is this item like the Bible? _____

Read **MATTHEW 4:4**. What item did you choose? _____
How is this item like the Bible? _____

Read **PSALM 119:103**. What item did you choose? _____
How is this item like the Bible? _____

When students are finished, go through the handout, giving the group members a chance to share their thoughts and answers. Hold up the items as you discuss them. Below are some thoughts for your part of the discussion:

- Mirror—James 1:23-25: Allows us to see our reflection in light of what God wants us to look like. When we read about Him, we see the kind of people He wants us to become.
- Sword—Hebrews 4:12: God's Word is our weapon to fight against the lie of Satan and his demons.
- Seed—1 Peter 1:23: A seed is something that has life in it. When we plant it in our hearts, God's Word will bring life to us as well.
- Bottle of water—Ephesians 5:25-26: The only way to wash away the stain of the world is to daily wash in the Word of God. It cleanses our minds and purifies our hearts.
- Flashlight—Psalm 119:105: The Bible illuminates our lives and helps us see where to go.
- Lighter—Jeremiah 23:29: A fire burns with tremendous energy. God's Word is full of power to refine our lives.
- Hammer—Jeremiah 23:29: A hammer can break up very hard materials. The Bible can blast away at our hardness of heart and bondages that get in the way of our relationship with God.
- Milk—1 Peter 2:2: A baby survives on its mother's milk alone. We survive by the nourishment we receive as we read God's Word.
- Bread—Matthew 4:4: The food our soul needs is the Bible. We can't live apart from it.
- Honey—Psalm 119:103: The Bible isn't all rules and lists. It is a story of love and life. God's Word is sweet and satisfying.

Ask the students which one of these images is the most powerful to them and why they think this is so.

Option 2: Thirsty. For this option, you will need several boxes of soda crackers, a spray bottle filled with water, a water bottle for every student, and the story below. Begin by reminding students that the Bible is God's Word to us—His unique revelation in which He tells us what He likes and what He wants for His followers. However, if we've grown up in church, we can sometimes take the Bible for granted to the point that we think of it as just another book. In fact, the Bible is truly a powerful book, and it is able to reveal God to us even today.

Have a volunteer distribute several crackers to each student. Have the group members eat all of their crackers and then listen to the following story. Read slowly and deliberately—milk the adjectives for all they are worth to really make students thirsty.

> The sun blistered down on the dry, heat-cracked desert floor. The faint screech of a hawk drifted on the steamy, warm air currents. Through his scratchy eyes, Brandon could glimpse the barren, distant horizon as he agonized his way forward, crawling painfully toward it. The heat rose from the ground in wavy, invisible streams, leaving a teasing impression of water without an ounce of moisture anywhere around. Stale and thick, his arid mouth ached for liquid—something, anything, to quench his searing, parched throat. In this desperate, desolate place, even the drinking fountain at school sounded good. Brandon collapsed, his dehydrated muscles straining forward with a last drop of strength. *Water!* He thought. *Water! I need water . . .*

Stop and ask the students if anyone has ever been lost in a hot desert without any water. No one probably has. Then ask if anyone has ever been really, really thirsty. Having just eaten dry salted crackers, they probably are right now! Keep driving them toward thirst as you ask them if anyone hates it when their mouth is so dry they can barley swallow. Have any of them ever had their tongue feel so thick and dry it almost choked them?

Explain that the Bible says God's Word is more necessary to us than food. Our physical body needs to eat and drink, or it will die. Likewise, our spiritual life—our relationship with God—will begin to whither unless we come to Him through His Word on a regular basis. We need God's Word as much as Brandon needs some water. Continue reading the story as follows:

> Brandon passed out in the sand and was baking away in the merciless desert oven. The heat had sapped him of all energy to continue. He thought it was over. Then it happened. It began to rain. [Mist the group members with the water bottle, and continue doing so as you read the rest of this story.] Gentle, peaceful, pristine droplets of H_2O came floating down. Quiet, easy streams of crystal clear liquid began to wash away the desert heat and renew his energy and strength. With each drop, he became more and more refreshed until at last he was able to rise to his feet. He opened his mouth to drink in all he could— he wanted every bit of that fresh, cool, restoring flow.

Distribute the bottled water to students and read aloud Psalm 119:25-32. Explain that Psalm 119 is the longest chapter in the Bible. Over and over again, it tells us of the blessings that God's laws—His Word—brings to us. Without God, we are like Brandon, lost in a dry, parched desert. But God didn't leave us there to die. He gave us water that will renew our strength and energize our spirit: the Bible. Distribute Bibles and have students reread the passage to locate ways in which the Bible can help them. Below are some suggestions for discussion:

- God's Word preserves our life (see verse 25).
- God's Word strengthens us when we are sorrowful and weary (see verse 28).
- God's Word keeps us from being deceitful (see verse 29).
- God's Word keeps us from being ashamed (see verse 31).
- God's Word sets our hearts free (see verse 32).

Conclude by stating that because the Bible is holy and a unique revelation from God, it will bless our lives and help us to live life the way God intended.

APPLY

Option 1: A Chapter a Day. For this option, you will need several gift Bibles and bookmarks. Ahead of time, bookmark the Bibles to the Gospel of Luke.

Begin by stating to the group that you are going to challenge them to read one chapter of the Bible every day for the next 24 days. In particular, you would like for them to begin by reading the Gospel of Luke. State that as they read the Bible, you believe God will reveal Himself and His great love to them.

Distribute Bibles and explain that you've bookmarked these Bibles to the Gospel of Luke. State that this is one of the four books in the Bible that specifically talks about Jesus' life on earth, His death and His resurrection. There is no pressure and no candy prize if they take the challenge to read one chapter a day, but they will receive the rich and incomparable blessing of getting a clearer glimpse of the Lord who created them and cares for them.

Close with this prayer from Ephesians 1:17 and Psalm 119:18:

Lord, as these students commit to reading Your Word, I pray that You would give them a spirit of wisdom and revelation so that they may know You better. Open their eyes that they might see wonderful things in Your Word. Amen.

Follow up with any visitors, making sure to get their names and contact information. Call them during the week to encourage them to keep on reading (and to come back to youth group!).

Option 2: Like a Box of Chocolates. For this option, you will need your Bible, a small box of chocolates (such as Whitman's® or See's® candies), index cards, pens or pencils, and several gift Bibles to give to students who do not have a Bible at home.

Explain that the Bible isn't about knowing facts; it is about experiencing God. His Word is *life*! Have student volunteers read John 20:31 and John 17:3 to the group. Continue by stating that the Word of God gives us life because it reveals Jesus to us—to have Him is to have life. However, it's not enough to just hear the Bible being taught in church. If they really want to know God and sense His presence, they need to commit to a *daily* devotional time, which includes reading His Word.

State that having a Bible is much like having a box of chocolates. Hold up the box, and then continue by explaining that we can smell the candy (take a nice, long whiff), look on the back to see what kind of chocolates are in the box (read aloud whatever kinds are listed), and even see the actual chocolates (take off the lid, walk around the room and hold the box in their faces), but what good does that do? The real joy comes from opening the box and eating one! (Eat a chocolate and enjoy every savory bite—make the students drool.) It is exactly the same with the Bible. We can polish the cover, state all the biblical books in the proper order, and parade it around as a Christian accessory. But unless we open it and taste its contents, we will never really experience the life it can bring.

Pass out one index card and a pen or pencil to each student. Challenge the students to start reading their Bibles every day. Have them take a few moments to decide how many chapters or verses a day they will begin reading, starting tomorrow, and then write down what they decide on the index card. Next, have them decide the best time of day for them to read the Bible, and have them write that down on the card. Finally, have them choose a book of the Bible to begin reading. You can suggest the psalms or the Gospels, but let them decide. Explain that they are the only ones who will see this card. Have them take it home to remind them to read it every day.

Distribute the Bibles to those in the group who do not have one and then close in prayer, asking God to help them keep their commitments to read His Word daily.

REFLECT

The following short devotions are for the students to reflect on and answer during the week. You can make a copy of these pages and distribute them to your class or download and print them from **www.gospellight.com/uncommon/jh_ the_armor_of_god.zip**.

1—UNWRAP IT!

Flip to Proverbs 2:1-5 and find out what happens when you search for wisdom from God's Word.

Imagine that for your birthday you receive the gift you've wanted for months (or even years). Different people are into different things, so for you the "best gift ever" might be a new Xbox, a new pair of shoes or a new phone. Whatever the gift is, it is awesome!

Then imagine that you never bother to unwrap it. You carry it around, showing it off to everybody—even the class bully, Marie, just to make her jealous—but keep it locked up tight in its box, shiny and new . . . and useless.

God's gift to His people is His Word, the Bible, and it truly is the best gift ever because it reveals what the God of the universe wants us to know about Him. But we can't find out what He wants us to know if we never bother to open it.

When was the last time (outside of church) that you unwrapped God's gift, His Word?

_____
_____
_____

What is the most interesting thing you've found out about God in the Bible?

_____
_____
_____

Read Proverbs 2:1-5 one more time and then rewrite it in your own words. Do you believe this promise? Why or why not?

_____
_____
_____

2—HOW WILL YOU RESPOND?

Check out Ephesians 1:17 to see what you need to know God better.

God has been pretty busy since He decided to create the universe, doing all kinds of amazing things so we can know Him. He made a world that not only provides for all our needs but also is gorgeous beyond description. He designed a plan to make right all of the things we have done wrong. He sent His Son to defeat sin and evil by dying—and then raised Him from the grave to defeat death, too! He inspired different people in different places and different centuries to write down what He revealed to them about Himself, His people and His plan for the world (we call these writings the Bible).

But He wasn't done yet! God also sent the Holy Spirit to lead us into a deeper knowledge of Him. Here's the thing: God's Word is an important part of the Holy Spirit's work in our lives. When we read and study the Bible, the Holy Spirit continues God's work of revealing Himself to us.

Spend a few minutes today thinking about all the incredible things God has done to make Himself known to you. List a few of these below.

_____

_____

_____

Now think about what actions you can take to respond to Him. Will reading and studying His Word be a part of your response? What about spending time with the Spirit in prayer? Write what you will do below.

_____

_____

_____

3—DON'T FORGET

Skedaddle on over to James 1:23-25 and give it a read. Without looking in a mirror, how would you describe your face?

- ❑ Needs some work. I haven't been hit with an ugly stick, but I've been in the same room with one.
- ❑ Not too shabby. There are a couple things I'd change if I could, but it doesn't make me want to run screaming into the night.

❏ It will do. Everything seems to be in the right place and in working
    order, so I can't complain.
❏ Lookin' good! It's hard to be this hot and stay humble.

Now find a mirror and see if you were right. You probably were, because even
though you weren't looking, you've seen yourself many times before and remember what you look like. Just like you don't forget your face when you walk
away from a mirror, James 1:23-25 says that you shouldn't forget to obey
God's Word after you've read it. What have you read lately from the Bible that
you can put into practice today?

_____
_____
_____
_____
_____

What can you do in the future to remind yourself to put into practice what
you read in the Bible?

_____
_____
_____
_____
_____

4—HOLY, NOT MAGICAL

Open up that Bible you have to 2 Timothy 3:16 and find out what God's Word
is good for.

Derek is on the basketball team. Before every game, he puts on his lucky
socks, ties his sneakers left-over-right in double knots and says Philippians 4:13
three times: "I can do all things through Christ who gives me strength." He's
convinced that these pre-game rituals increase his team's chances of winning.

Poor Derek. It's great that he has memorized such an encouraging verse
of Scripture, but someone should tell him that the Bible is holy—that means
"set apart for God's purposes"—not magical. According to the apostle Paul's
letter to his young friend Timothy, God's Word is useful "for teaching, rebuking, correcting and training in righteousness" . . . not for getting God on our

side before a b-ball game! God has given us the Holy Bible to make us holy, not to bring us luck.

What do you think Paul means when he says the Bible is useful for "training in righteousness"?

_____
_____
_____
_____

In what ways does the Bible make us holy?

_____
_____
_____
_____

How are you using God's Word in your everyday life?

_____
_____
_____
_____

THE BIBLE IS TRUE

THE BIG IDEA
The Bible, the sword of the Spirit in our spiritual arsenal, is a reliable revelation of who God is and what He wants for our lives.

SESSION AIMS
In this session, you will guide students to (1) understand that accuracy determines reliability; (2) establish reasons for the accuracy and reliability of the Bible; and (3) help them confidently believe that when they read the Bible, they are actually reading God's Word.

THE BIGGEST VERSE
"All Scripture is God-breathed and is useful for teaching, rebuking, correcting and training in righteousness" (2 Timothy 3:16).

OTHER IMPORTANT VERSES
Psalm 22:1,14-18; Ezekiel 26; Micah 5:2; Matthew 2:1-6; Luke 1:1-4; 21:5-6; John 14:26; 19:1-42; Hebrews 4:12; 1 Peter 3:15; 2 Peter 1:21; 1 John 1:1

Note: Additional options and worksheets in 8$^{1}/_{2}$" x 11" format for this session are available for download at **www.gospellight.com/uncommon/jh_the_armor_of_god.zip**.

STARTER

Option 1: Which Is More Accurate? For this option, you will need your Bible, 10 to 12 items that vary in their degree of accuracy (for example, a dictionary, a weather report, a map, a watch, a teen magazine, an encyclopedia—the more creative the better), five sheets of paper, a felt-tip marker and masking tape. Ahead of time, write the numbers 1 through 5 on the paper (one number per paper). Tape the papers to the wall 3 to 4 feet apart in numerical order in an area where students can move underneath the numbers.

Greet students and welcome them to this session on the armor of God. Remind them how last week they learned about the uniqueness of the Bible. This week, you will be talking to them about why they can trust the Bible to be reliable. Hold up your Bible, and continue to share that if they are going to base their lives on the words of this book and use it to effectively battle the attacks of the enemy, it's important for them to know why they believe it to be true.

Ask the group what makes something reliable. Tell them that you have a little reliability survey that you want them to take right now. Have students stand up. Point to the numbers on the wall and explain that these numbers are a scale. Number 1 is for the lowest, least reliable items, while number 5 is for the highest, most reliable items. You will be holding up some items, and they will need to move and stand under the number that shows how reliable they think the information is in this item. Hold up each item, and allow students enough time to move under their numbers. To create more movement, vary the items so that you have an accurate item followed by a not-so-accurate item.

After you've surveyed all the items, discuss which items were the most reliable and why they were the most reliable. Allow time for students to respond, and then discuss the following questions:

- How would you determine if something is accurate? (*Consider the source, what other people say about its accuracy, and its track record of being true.*)

- Why is it so important that the Bible be accurate? (*Because our whole eternity is staked on whether or not what the Bible teaches is correct.*)

- Why is it important to know what we believe? (*So we can effectively wield the sword of the Spirit in spiritual battles and resist the enemy's attacks.*)

Conclude by explaining that because we are basing our eternal lives on this book, it's important that we know why we believe it to be accurate and reliable. That's what we're going to look at today—why we can trust that the Bible is a reliable revelation of who God is and what He wants for our lives.

Option 2: Rope Swing. For this option, you will need your Bible, two strong hooks, two 15-foot pieces of thick rope, a 3-foot piece of yarn, a 3-foot piece of dental floss, two plastic tarps, lots of shaving cream, duct tape, plenty of towels, a yard stick and prizes.

Mount the hooks into the ceiling of your room and tie a rope securely to each one. (Note: If your church has a playground with chin-up bars, you can tie the ropes to the highest bars and do this game outside. Your pastor and maintenance crew would probably prefer this!) The hook will need to support the weight of the students, so make sure to test it to prevent any mishaps. Place a plastic tarp under each rope, using duct tape around the edges to keep it in place. Squirt a tall pile of shaving cream on each tarp directly under the rope. Measure the pile to make sure each is the same height. Students will be swinging on the rope across the tarp, trying to avoid the shaving cream.

Divide the group into two teams. Have each group stand next to the rope areas. Tell the groups that the object of this activity is to get their whole team across this dangerous puddle and back again without any mishaps. The winning team will be the one whose pile is the highest after all the team members have crossed, so they want to get across without touching the shaving cream.

Have each team line up next to their rope area. Select one team member from each team to be the rope retriever. This person will be responsible for swinging or pulling the rope back to the next team member, and he or she does not have to cross. At your signal, let the game begin. (You may want to play loud, upbeat music for this game, as it tends to heighten the intensity and fun.) Each team member must get all the way across before anyone can start back again. Once the whole team is across, each team member must get back to the other side. When both teams are finished, have everyone sit down. Measure the height of each pile and award the winning team with a prize.

After the game is over, hold up your Bible and explain that last week they learned about the uniqueness of the Bible—that this book, the weapon in our spiritual arsenal, is God's written revelation of Himself. It's the specific way He has chosen to tell us what He's like and what He wants for us. But how do we know that the Bible is really true? State that the students just risked their lives in a near-death experience—okay, maybe not near-death, but definitely a close shave (ha! ha!)—to cross the tarp. They relied on the rope to do that. Explain that there might have been a few doubts among the group, but those doubts were overcome when everyone got across. Hold up the yarn and ask students if they would have tried to swing across on the yarn. (*The answer is no.*) Hold up the dental floss and ask if the would have tried to swing across using the floss. (*Definitely not.*) Ask students why they considered the rope to be reliable. (*Some answers might be that they've seen other people go across on similar ropes or that it looked strong enough to support them.*)

Conclude by explaining that when we think about the Bible, there are some clear reasons to believe that it is reliable as well. We can trust that the Bible is a reliable revelation of who God is and what He wants for our lives. Today, we're going to look at some of the reasons why.

MESSAGE

Option 1: Solid Steps. For this option, you will need several Bibles, 20 large Styrofoam® cups, 9 soup-sized cans, a felt-tip marker and a copy of "Solid Steps" (found on the following page). The cup will need to be large enough to cover the soup-sized can (which will act as a support underneath it) without being so big that it crumples over the can when stepped on, so *test it first*! A student will be walking on the upside down cups, trying to guess which ones have a support underneath and which ones do not.

Ahead of time, use the marker to number the cups 1 to 20. Fit the cans inside the cups that have the numbers 1-9 written on them. Make a path to walk on by placing all of the cups upside down in a random order (mix the numbers up and the cans—some with can support and some without) at the front of the room where students can see.

Begin by reminding the group that last week we discussed how the Bible is a one-of-a-kind revelation of God to us. It is His Word that tells us what He is like and what He wants for our lives. Read 2 Timothy 3:16 aloud and explain that many people doubt whether or not the Bible is something they can trust and whether it really is God's Word. These people have trouble believing that something as ordinary as these written pages could contain eternal truth from a living God. They believe that somehow His words must have been changed and that the Bible is not really as inspired as it claims to be.[1]

Continue by stating that there are many clear, solid reasons to believe what the Bible says about itself—reasons much more solid than "just because." The Bible can stand up under the toughest questions. It can endure any test to verify its reliability. How can we test the accuracy and reliability of the Bible? Point to the cups, and say something like the following:

What you see here is a reliability test path. Each cup represents a step we can take to test the Bible's reliability. As we walk along the path, we

Solid Steps to Test the Bible's Reliability (Numbers 1 Through 9)

1. The Bible itself claims to be God's Word—more than 3,000 times the people who wrote down the words of the Bible claimed to be speaking not their words but God's. That's why you read in the Bible over and over again, "The LORD says . . ." (see 2 Samuel 23:2; Jeremiah 1:7,9; Ezekiel 2:7).

2. Jesus Himself quotes the Bible as authoritative (see Matthew 5:18; Luke 24:44).

3. The apostles quoted the Bible as authoritative (see Acts 4:24-25; Galatians 3:8).

4. There are hundreds of fulfilled prophecies in the Bible. For one example, see Micah 5:2, written around 700 BC, and Matthew 2:1-6, the foretelling of the Messiah's birthplace, which was fulfilled accurately around AD 4.

5. There is a seamless unity in the Bible (a common theme and message from Genesis to Revelation), even though the Bible was written over a period of 1,500 years by 40 different people).

6. Archeological evidence can verify the places and people mentioned in the Bible, both Hebrew and other nationalities.

7. The Bible has remained a powerful influence in the world for thousands of years. People read it, write about it, sing about it, depict it in art and drama and study it.

8. Even in the face of tremendous persecution, the Bible has never been completely destroyed. It has been miraculously preserved time and time again.

9. The Bible has the power to change your life, if you sincerely seek the One who gave it to you—God. His Word can change your life forever!

Weak Steps to Test the Bible's Reliability (Numbers 10 Through 19)

10. The Bible looks pretty impressive because it's thick and has gold edges.

11. The Bible is old, so it must be worth something.

12. The Bible is on the *New York Times* bestseller list.

13. The Bible can make you seem smart and is good to carry around.

14. The Bible is a pretty good place to get some advice if you need it.

15. The people who wrote the Bible were really important at some time in history.

16. The Bible is hard to understand, so it must be an important book.

17. The Bible has some really interesting stories in it.

18. Your teacher said not to believe it—so it must be true!

19. The Bible always makes you feel sleepy, so I guess it helps keep you stay peaceful.

will find some steps that are solid and others that are weak. Solid steps give us a place to stand strong in our faith about the Bible actually being God's Word. Solid steps are the bits of evidence and logic that uphold the Bible's reliability. These are the steps we want to choose when looking for answers to our questions about God's Word. These strong steps can stand up to heavy pressure [stand on a supported cup] and close scrutiny. Weak steps will crush beneath even a little bit of pressure [stand on an unsupported cup]. Your job is simply to get to the end of the path by choosing which steps you're going to take.

Choose a volunteer and have that person begin by standing on a cup with a soup can supporting it so it will not be crushed. As the volunteer chooses his or her next step, have that person call out the number on the cup. After he or she takes a step, find that number on the "Solid Steps" handout and read the information aloud to the group. If the volunteer chooses a cup that is solid, he or she will be able to step across and continue; if not, then the cup will be crushed and that student can sit down. At that point, another student can either start from the first cup and retrace the previous student's steps, or that student can start from the crushed cup and move forward.

When the volunteer has reached the other side, you will have covered eight solid reasons we can trust the Bible to be accurate. Thank the group members for taking such wild risks on your reliability path and conclude by explaining that the most important test for them to consider now is if they will open their hearts to the words of this Book and let God speak to them. Read 1 John 1:1 and challenge students with the fact that if they seek God with an honest, open heart, He will open their eyes and they will experience the power of God through His Word to change them—forever!

Option 2: Be a Scribe. For this option, you will need several Bibles, classical music, a way to play the music to the group, sheet music of a classical song (if it matches the music that you are going to play, great, but if not, that's okay), a clay jar, parchment paper, copies of "Be a Scribe" (found on the next page), felt-tip markers, a stack of letters and a lighter. Ahead of time, write out Micah 5:2 on the parchment paper, and then roll it up and place it in the clay jar.

Begin by reminding the students that they have just learned that accuracy determines reliability. If something is found to be accurate, people depend on it to be reliable. When we say the Bible is accurate and reliable, we are saying that we believe it to be God's Word, and therefore we can depend on it. There

BE A SCRIBE

Copy the following verse from Genesis 1:1 written in Hebrew, the original language of the Old Testament. Be as accurate as possible.

בְּרֵאשִׁית בָּרָא אֱלֹהִים אֵת הַשָּׁמַיִם וְאֵת הָאָרֶץ׃

_____

_____

_____

_____

_____

_____

_____

_____

_____

_____

_____

are a lot of good reasons why we can make this claim—good, logical reasons. Let's consider some of them.

Distribute Bibles and have one of the students read 2 Timothy 3:16. Explain that the Bible itself claims to be God's Word. In this verse, we read that every word is "inspired." This word in the original language of the New Testament literally means "God-breathed." Hold up the sheet music. Explain that when we listen and understand how beautiful and complex classical music is, we begin to see why composers such as Bach and Mozart are often called "inspired."

Play a two or three minute selection from the classical music. Continue by stating that these composers' music is amazing—it is far beyond any normal musical talent or ability. This can also be said about some of today's musicians. Ask the group to list any musicians they like who they would consider to be "inspired." Ask them why they selected those particular musicians—what makes him or her inspired?

Hold up your Bible and explain that when we say the Bible is inspired, we are saying much more than the fact that the writers had a good idea and wrote it down. We are saying that the *words of the book themselves came from God*; they were breathed out by God and are not a product of human ideas but a divine revelation. The words of this unique book are God's *inspiration*.

Continue by asking the students how we can prove this. Explain that the first reason has to do with *fulfilled prophecy.* The Bible gives hundreds of prophecies about events hundreds of years before they happened. Many of these referred to the coming of the Messiah or to the rise and fall of various nations, and we can go back in history and see that these prophecies happened just as God said they would. Share the following verses with students as specific examples of fulfilled prophecies, making sure to emphasize the dates that the prophecy was given and then fulfilled:

- *Prophecy:* The foretelling of the Messiah's birthplace to be in Bethlehem
  Old Testament prophecy: Micah 5:2, written around 700 BC
  Prophecy fulfilled in the New Testament: Matthew 2:1-6, which states the Messiah was born in Bethlehem around AD 4

- *Prophecy:* The detailed foretelling of the Messiah's suffering
  Old Testament prophecy: Psalm 22:1,14-18, written around 1000 BC; Isaiah 52:1–53:12, written around 700 BC
  Prophecy fulfilled in the New Testament: John 19:1-42, which states the Messiah was beaten and crucified around AD 33

- *Prophecy:*The foretelling of the destruction of the ancient city of Tyre
  Old Testament prophecy: Ezekiel 26, written around 580 BC
  Prophecy fulfilled: Alexander the Great destroyed the city in 332 BC

- *Prophecy:* The temple in Jerusalem would be destroyed
  New Testament prophecy: Luke 21:5-6, where Jesus prophesies the destruction of the Temple while still living on earth (spoken around AD 30)
  Prophecy fulfilled: The Romans tore the Temple down in AD 70

Sum up the main point by stating there are hundreds of verses just like these throughout the Bible. The accuracy of these prophecies point to the reliability of the entire Bible. What it said would happen did happen. So, whoever inspired these words must have known the future—maybe someone like God!

Continue by stating that the second reason we can know the Bible is accurate is that *the scribes who copied it followed strict rules*. Explain that some people say God originally inspired the Bible at the time it was written, but that now it has all changed and is full of errors. In fact, detailed scribes copied the Bible by hand for many years, and the copying rules for these scribes were very strict. Distribute a felt-tip pen and copies of "Be a Scribe" to each student. Have them copy the Hebrew text as accurately as they can.

As they are finishing up, explain that the scribes who copied the Old Testament, which was written in Hebrew similar to what they just wrote down, counted and recounted each line to make sure they had not left one single stroke out. If anything was found to be different than the original, the copy was destroyed! (Take an extra handout and crumple it up to emphasize the point.) In this way, the scribes were assured that they had letter-perfect copies. This was proved true in 1947 when a young shepherd boy found a group of clay jars containing portions of the Bible that had been copied around AD 150. When these pages were compared with other copies dating to almost 1,000 years later, the two manuscripts were found to be almost identical.

Hold up the letters and state that the New Testament is different because it was a collection of letters that weren't put into one book until a few hundred years after Jesus' resurrection. However, there are more than 5,000 parts or whole books of the Greek New Testament that survive today. When compared side by side, all of the copies support each other and fit together with consistency. This is partly due to the fact that the original letters were written within the lifetimes of the disciples. They didn't wait until years had passed before they wrote down the things they had seen Jesus do.

Read Luke 1:1-4 and 1 John 1:1. Explain that before Jesus went back to heaven, He promised that the Holy Spirit would come to direct the disciples in their teachings about Him. Now read John 14:26 and 2 Peter 1:21. State that these disciples, moved by the Holy Spirit, wrote down God-inspired teachings so that the followers of Jesus could become all that they were supposed to be. The first Christians, their churches and the Early Church leaders accepted these letters as the inspired Word of God.

At this point, some students might be wondering why it took several hundred years to put the New Testament together. To illustrate the reason, light a corner of the stack of letters on fire, but be ready to blow it out before it gets very big. Explain that the Christians endured tremendous persecution beginning with the Roman emperor Nero in AD 60 that lasted through AD 330, when the Roman emperor Constantine declared Christianity a lawful religion. During that time, Christians were tortured and killed, and many copies of the New Testament letters were burned. Yet despite the pressure of persecution, the Bible survived. (Blow out the flame.) After the persecution died out, the Church leaders put the New Testament letters together in a public, open way—not in some secret room with only two or three people around. The letters were carefully scrutinized, fiercely debated and finally compiled into what we now call the New Testament. (Hold up your Bible—again!)

Explain that there are several other reasons to believe in the reliability of the Bible. The first is the fact that Jesus quoted the Bible as authoritative. A second is that there is a perfect unity of message among the books of the Bible, even though about 40 different people wrote the books over a period of 1,500 years in 3 different languages on 3 different continents. A third reason for the reliability of Scripture is that there is an avalanche of archaeological evidence to confirm the people and places mentioned in the Bible. The fourth reason is the fact that the Bible has endured throughout the centuries as one of the most influential and sought-out books ever written.

DIG

Option 1: Hot Seat. For this option, you will need a prepared pastor or church leader (other than yourself, of course). Ahead of time, explain to the pastor or leader that he or she will be placed in the "hot seat" for students to question him or her about why that person believes the Bible is the Word of God.

To give students an opportunity to practice sharing some of the information they have learned during this session, have them pair up and take turns explaining to each other why the Bible is accurate and reliable. Have one student from each pair take the side of a critic, while the other defends the Bible's claims to be God's Word. After they have discussed their views, have them switch roles and do it again. The goal is to give students a chance to articulate for themselves some of the reasons they find most compelling to support their beliefs. After both students have tried both roles, discuss the following as a group:

- What was the hardest part of criticizing the reliability of the Bible?
- What was the hardest part of defending the reliability of the Bible?
- What, in your opinion, are some of the most convincing evidences for the Bible's reliability?

As you ask these questions, consider what are some of the strongest doubts you are hearing. This should let you know what really hit home and give you an idea where students are with their own doubts and questions. Encourage students that seeking answers in an honest way never offends God. In fact, He welcomes all who seek Him with respectful faith (see Psalm 25:14).

Ask students if they can "prove" the Bible is God's Word. The answer is no—because the Bible can only be understood through the power of the Holy Spirit. They will be able to present convincing points that leave little room for doubt, but it will still comes down to God opening people's eyes to His truth. Stress that we are not called to do the work of the Holy Spirit to convict and convince others. We are called to be witnesses, telling others what we know to be true. To conclude, invite the pastor or leader to come in and take the hot seat. Give students a chance to ask questions about the Bible's reliability. Hopefully, they will gain not only another layer of evidence but also the assurance that other people they respect are convinced the Bible is the Word of God.

Option 2: Sal's Story. For this option, you will need the following story, a whiteboard and a dry erase marker. Read aloud this story—and enunciate!

Sal was excited about again seeing his best friend. Jarod had moved away six weeks ago, and since then Sal had been a little less occupied— okay, he was bored. With spare time on his hands, he had begun to go to youth group with his older sister, Jenna. At church, he learned that the Bible is the Word of God and that he could rely on it to teach him what he needed to know about God and His plan for his life. Sal had begun a daily Bible reading plan and was enjoying his devotional time with God. Every day there was something new to read, which made him feel closer to his heavenly Father.

Suddenly, the doorbell rang. Sal flew down the stairs and nearly flung the front door off its hinges. There stood Jarod, same blue sweat-shirt and faded jeans as always. His shoelaces were tucked down inside his shoes and his scooter jetted out of its case, dangling precariously from Jarod's shoulder. After the initial greetings, they went up to Sal's room to hang out. Jarod set his things down and quickly noticed Sal's Bible sitting on his desk. "Don't tell me you're reading that!" he said. "It's just a bunch of stories that have nothing to do with real life."

Feeling a little intimidated, Sal mumbled something about it be-longing to Jenna when he suddenly felt the Holy Spirit tugging on his heart. Reading the Bible had totally changed Sal's walk with God. He loved it and felt uncomfortable pretending that he didn't care.

"Actually," Sal began, "I have been reading that book. I read it every day, and it has really helped me grow closer to God."

"Oh, no, not you!" Jarod gasped. "I mean, the Bible is for people who don't have a brain. It's full of mistakes and contradictions. Every-one knows that."

Stop the story at this point and discuss the following questions:

- Have you ever been too intimidated to let others know that you read your Bible?
- What would you do if you were in Sal's shoes?
- What kind of evidence could you bring up to show the Bible's reliability?

List the group's responses to the last item on the whiteboard. Be ready to prompt them, as this is likely to be new information to at least some of them. Conclude by stating that we never have to feel embarrassed that we believe the Bible is what it claims to be—God's Word. We can tell people the evidence we discussed earlier, and we can share our own experiences and how reading the Bible has changed us. God is able to convince minds and convict hearts that the words of the Book are really from Him.

APPLY

Option 1: Sharing the Word. For this option, you will need nothing but a heart that longs to see students pursue God. Explain to the group members that when considering the reliability of the Bible, they will be faced with its bold message of sold-out faith in God. In other words, if they believe the Bible really is His Word, they will be compelled to do something with its message. The Bible will affect their daily life.

Have students break into groups of three to four. Read 1 Peter 3:15 and explain that there is no way they will be ready to give an answer for this hope if they haven't spent time reading and talking with the reason for their hope—Jesus! Through prayer and Bible reading, they can be ready to tell others why they have the joy they have, why their lives are blessed even when things are hard, and why they have high hopes and strong faith. Give each group an opportunity to pray for each other. Conclude with prayer, asking God to increase students' opportunities to share the Bible with those around them.

Option 2: Bookmark Memory Verses 1. For this option, you will need copies of "Bookmark Memory Verses" (included in the worksheet files available for download) and breath mints. Ahead of time, copy the bookmarks onto card stock and cut them apart. Prepare to give out the bookmark for 2 Timothy 3:16 during this session, and save the rest for the following sessions.

For this option, you will have the students begin a Bible memorization project. For the next five weeks, they will be memorizing one verse per session. These verses are printed as bookmarks, and you can print them all at once, cut them apart and distribute them one by one over the course of this series. As always, providing motivation such as a contest, prizes or certificates is effective in getting students moving. You can award a prize every session or at the end of the series if all the verses are memorized, or do both!

Distribute the bookmarks for 2 Timothy 3:16 and have students read the verse aloud several times. Explain that this session's memory verse is one we have been referring to throughout this session. The key word in this verse is the word "inspired." It tells us that the words of the Bible are God-breathed, full of His life and power.

Distribute a breath mint to each student and have the group members eat the mint and then blow air out of their mouths. State that they should be able to feel the stream of air moving out from their mouths. This will give them an idea of what 2 Timothy 3:16 means when it says the Bible is "God-breathed." God gave us His Word so we could come to know Him and His plan for our lives.

Before you dismiss the session, remind the students of their daily Bible reading challenge. If they haven't been reading at all, encourage them to start today. Close in prayer, asking for God's blessing and grace to work in their lives.

REFLECT

The following short devotions are for the students to reflect on and answer during the week. You can make a copy of these pages and distribute them to your class or download and print them from **www.gospellight.com/uncommon/jh_ the_armor_of_god.zip**.

1—PROBLEMS AND ANSWERS

Track down the Spirit-given words of 1 Corinthians 2:13-14.

Think about your math book for a minute (come on, it won't kill you!). If yours is like many other textbooks, it has a section with the answers at the back so you can check to see if you've solved the math problems correctly. But which is more valuable—the problems or the answers? The answers *are* pretty great, but the whole point of a math book is to help you learn how to do math. And you learn how to do math by solving problems, not by peeking at the answers.

In what way do you think the Bible might be like your math book?

_____

_____

_____

Which do you think is more valuable—the answers the Bible gives or the problems it gives you to solve? Why?

_____

_____

_____

The Bible is God's trustworthy textbook for teaching us how to live and love Him. Say a short prayer thanking Him for this awesome how-to guide!

2—NOW THAT'S SHARP!

Look sharp! Read Hebrews 4:12 to find out how sharp the Word of God is.

Mel and her mom don't get along because Mel thinks her mom treats her like a baby. She never lets Mel ride around with high-school friends or stay at the mall past eight o'clock on Friday night, and she makes Mel finish her homework before doing anything fun. Plus, Mel has to make her bed *every* morning or she gets dishwasher duty for a whole week! It's so not fair.

Lately, Mel has been giving Mom the silent treatment—only talking when absolutely necessary and making those few words as hostile as possible. But then, at youth group this week, Mel read Ephesians 6:1-3: "Children, obey your parents in the Lord, for this is right. 'Honor your father and mother'—which is the first commandment with a promise—'so that it may go well with you and that you may enjoy long life on the earth.'" How do you think Mel feels when she reads those verses?

❑ Guilty and ashamed
❑ Determined to change her attitude
❑ Hopeful because of God's promise
❑ All of the above

Have you ever read a verse or passage of Scripture that cut straight to your heart and felt like it was written just for you? If so, what happened?

_____

_____

_____

3—KNOW WHO TO TRUST

Check out 1 John 1:1. Sounds like he knows what he's talking about, huh?

Here's a brainy phrase for you: "apostolic witness." Now you can sound really smart at the cafeteria lunch table. You'll sound even smarter if you know what it means. "Apostolic witness" simply means that the accounts of Jesus we have in the New Testament are based on the witness of His earliest followers, the apostles.

We believe the writer of 1 John was one of those apostles, and in the first line of this letter he tells his readers that he not only heard and saw Jesus, but also that he touched the risen Lord after He was resurrected from the dead. Holy moley!

Do you think the apostolic witness of the New Testament is trustworthy? Why or why not? (It's okay if you're not sure yet.)

_____

_____

_____

_____

What are some questions you have about the Bible's trustworthiness?

_____
_____
_____

What are two things you will do this week to get some answers about the Bible?

_____
_____
_____

Your youth leader or pastor can help you work through your doubts and concerns about the Bible, so put him or her on your list!

4—AS IT IS WRITTEN

So, you've read Matthew 2:1-6 before? Well, read it again.

The story of the wise men, or magi, is familiar to all of us who love Christmas. A few (maybe three, maybe more) genius dudes from east of Judea followed a new star that, according to their genius calculations, was the sign of a new and powerful king. It made sense in their minds to visit the reigning king of Judea, Herod, because he would probably know about a new king, right?

Wrong. To find out what he needed to know, Herod asked the geniuses in Jerusalem. Where did they look for the answers? The Bible! Think about how amazing that is! They needed to know where the Messiah, God's Anointed One, would be born, so they cracked open God's Word to find out what the prophets had foretold.

What prophecy did the geniuses in Jerusalem give to Herod?

_____
_____
_____

How does this show that the Bible is inspired by God?

_____
_____
_____

Scripture really is *that* awesome.

THE BIBLE IS EVERLASTING

THE BIG IDEA
Nothing can stop God's Word—it will endure forever!

SESSION AIMS
In this session, you will guide students to (1) realize how God kept His message alive even through tremendous opposition; (2) understand the indestructible nature of the Bible's message; and (3) feel confident that the power of God's Word is at work in them today.

THE BIGGEST VERSE
"But the word of the Lord stands forever. And this was the word that was preached to you" (1 Peter 1:25).

OTHER IMPORTANT VERSES
2 Kings 22:8–23:25; Psalm 19:7-11; Luke 11:28; John 1:1-2,14; 17:8,17; Romans 12:2; 15:4; 1 Corinthians 10:11; Colossians 3:16-17; 2 Timothy 3:16; Hebrews 4:12; James 1:22; 1 Peter 1:23-25

Note: Additional options and worksheets in 8¹/₂" x 11" format for this session are available for download at **www.gospellight.com/uncommon/jh_the_armor_of_god.zip**.

STARTER

Option 1: Dress-up Relay. For this option, you will need three sets of clothing (five to seven garments per set) for a dress-up relay (e.g., hats, big shoes, jackets, gloves, ties—the weirder the better), three bags, three used skateboards, and masking tape. You will be giving one of the skateboards away, so make sure it is used but valuable enough for students to want it. You can check with local skate parks, thrift stores or second-hand sport shops for possible donations or cheap prices. Ahead of time, place the sets of clothing in the bags and tie them shut. Also, tape two long, parallel lines about 30 feet apart (or as far apart as you can in your meeting area) on the floor. Students will be running from one line to the other.

Greet students and give them a chance to share something from their personal Bible reading during the week—a verse or maybe even a section that really stood out to them. This is a great way to show students that you respect and value their input. When students have had a chance to share, divide them into three teams and have each team sit on the floor. Instruct the teams to divide into two equal groups. Send one half of the team to sit behind one of the lines, and have the other half sit directly across from them behind the other line. Choose one of the lines and put a bag of clothes in front of each team.

Explain that you were going through your closet and thought you would bring in some hand-me-downs for the group. Hold up an undesirable article of clothing and say, "I hope they fit you and that you like them. These are clothes I really love, but the time has come for me to pass them on to you."

Instruct the teams sitting in front of the bags of clothes that when you give the signal, one team member will open his or her bag, dress in the clothes and then use the skateboard (standing, sitting or kneeling) to get across the room, where the other half of his or her team is waiting. At that point, the one who is dressed up must take off the clothes and hand them down to someone else on their team. That person will then dress and "skate"

Youth Leader Tip
Don't shoulder the burden of collecting resources. Ask parents and other group leaders to help you gather stuff. This will give you a lot more spiritual preparation time during the week.

back to the other side, repeating the dressing/undressing process until every-one has done it. The teams will be finished when students are sitting on the opposite side of where they started.

Hold up one of the wackier articles of clothing. Explain that hand-me-downs are unusual things. Sometimes you get really dorky stuff. Give the cloth-ing to someone in the group. Now hold up the give-away skateboard. State that sometimes, however, you get really cool stuff that you not only can use but also like! Give the skateboard to some lucky student (preferably someone who likes skateboarding).

Continue by stating that in some ways, the Bible is a hand-me-down. It has been passed from one generation to the next, sometimes at great cost. But the truth of God's Word is much more valuable than clothes or skateboards. It is a living revelation that is as powerful today as the day God inspired it. It is a weapon in our spiritual arsenal that can help us to defeat the attacks of the en-emy. Let students know that today you will be taking a look at this valuable hand-me-down from God!

Option 2: Digging for Treasure. For this option, you will need two big card-board boxes (dishwasher-sized if possible) and a wide assortment of used items such as clothes, toys, household items, fake jewelry, and so on. Make sure to have a few nicer items—things students would value—in the mix. You might be able to borrow these items from your church's second-hand store or donation barrel if you have one. Otherwise, ask parents and leaders involved in your jun-ior-high ministry to collect the items for you—they will not be damaged and can be returned. (A last resort would be a thrift store, but then you would have to buy the stuff.) Ahead of time, divide the used items and place them inside the boxes. Try to make sure that each box contains similar type things (for in-stance, both boxes have clothes, both have books, both have toys).

Greet students and talk about their week. Ask how their daily Bible reading is going and encourage them to stay committed to reading from God's Word every day. Remind the group that they have been studying the armor of God from Ephesians 6:10-18. This week, you and the group will continue to study the sword of the Spirit, or the Bible, which is their offensive weapon to defeat the spiritual darkness in this work.

Begin this week's session by selecting two teams of six to eight students. Have the teams come forward and place one box of used items in front of each team. Instruct the teams that at your signal, they will have two minutes to dig through their box and find the three most valuable items they can. What makes the item "valuable" is up to each team. At the end of the two minutes, the students who have been watching will judge which team was able to come up with the most valuable items. Signal a start, and time the teams accordingly.

When the teams have selected their three items, hold them up and have the students applaud for which set they think is better. Congratulate the winning team. Explain that in some ways the Bible is like the hand-me-downs they found in these boxes, and it takes a little effort to dig through and find the really good stuff. However, the Bible isn't a useless, unwanted give-away—it is a priceless revelation that God ensured would be passed on from one generation to the next so we could read it and know Him. It is our weapon of warfare to defeat the attacks of the enemy, which should make it a priceless item to us. Today, we're going to focus on the power of this indestructible hand-me-down—the Bible.

MESSAGE

Option 1: People of the Word. For this option, you will need your Bible, three adult volunteers (Church history buffs preferred), copies of "People of the Word" (found on the next page), copies of "Character Notes" (included in the worksheet files available for download), and pens or pencils. Ahead of time, assign a character role to each of the three adult volunteers and give them a copy of "Character Notes" to help them prepare. Simple costumes really enhance this, so consider using the following costume ideas:

Jerome:	Roman toga, unkempt appearance
Wycliffe:	College professor's robe and cap, long beard
Tyndale:	Long coat

Designate three separate areas for the volunteers to be stationed during this option. Note that for this option, students will be going from one character to the next to fill in the questions on their handouts, so the volunteers will want to be sure they can effectively answer at least those questions.

Begin by reminding the group members that they have learned how the Bible represents our sole weapon in our spiritual arsenal, how unique it is, and how reliable it is. This week, they are going to learn how *indestructible* it is. Read 1 Peter 1:23-25 and explain that the Bible and the people who valued it faced every type of opposition possible—from upset emperors, to fire, to floods, to prisons, to evil people in the Church . . . you name it. Since the time

PEOPLE OF THE WORD

JEROME

c. 347–420

1. When and where were you born?
2. What was your family life like?
3. Where did you go to school?
4. What did you study?
5. Was there a turning point in your commitment as a Christian?
6. What language did you study when you left Rome and spent four years in the desert?
7. What Pope did you work for?
8. What was your life's most important work?
9. Was your life's work well received?

JOHN WYCLIFFE

c. 1328–1384

1. What country were you from?
2. During what period of time did you live?
3. What were people like during this period?
4. Who were the educated people?
5. How did they treat the poor people?
6. How old were you when you left for college?
7. What college did you attend?
8. What bothered you about the church that existed during that time?
9. What was the church teaching that was not from the Bible?
10. Why did people believe the church leaders?
11. What was your solution to this problem?
12. How long did it take to make one copy of the Bible?
13. How did your translation get out to the people who lived during that time?
14. How did the monks try to get revenge on you 40 years after your death?

WILLIAM TYNDALE

c. 1494–1536

1. What was against the law in your day?
2. What school did you attend?
3. What job did you take after school?
4. What risk were you facing by translating the Bible into English?
5. Where did you move to finish your Bible work?
6. What new invention really helped your work go faster?
7. Where did you send the first shipment of Bibles?
8. What happened as a result?
9. Where did you live after that?
10. How did the authorities finally catch you?
11. Were you scared to die?
12. What were your last words?
13. What famous Bible was based in part on your translation work?

God gave His Word, Satan has used people to try to destroy this powerful weapon, but no one has ever succeeded. Why? Because the Bible is not an ordinary book—it is the living Word, inspired by God Almighty, and it will outlast even its fiercest enemy.

Continue by stating that today you thought they would like to meet some of the people from the past who have helped get the Bible into their hands. Distribute copies of "People of the Word" and pens or pencils. Have the adult leaders who have prepared the various roles come into the room and move to their designated areas. Divide students into three groups, and have one group talk with each leader. During the discussion time, the groups are to get the information requested on their handout. When everyone has had a chance to make the circuit, thank the volunteers and have the students return to their seats.

Go over the handout as a group and have the students volunteer to answer each question. When you are finished, reread 1 Peter 1:25 and explain that nothing can stop the Word of God because it is full of His very life. This is good news for us as Christians. We can rest assured that our lives are grounded on truth that can't be destroyed.

Option 2: Power of the Word. For this option, you will need several Bibles, a pitcher of water, a clear bowl of ice cubes, a teakettle, an oven mitt, a gas or electric burner, matches (if you're using a gas burner), a table, copies of "Power of the Word" (found on pages 135-136), and pens or pencils. Ahead of time, set up the table where students will be able to see you demonstrate the three states of matter. Place the kettle, burner (make sure you're close to an outlet if needed), pitcher of water and bowl of ice cubes on the table. (*Safety Note:* Make sure you have a fire extinguisher in your room for emergencies. Because this option involves fire, make sure it works so that you're prepared just in case you need to douse an ambitious flame!)

Turn on the burner to heat the water and explain that because the Word of God is a powerful weapon to defeat darkness in the world, Satan, our enemy,

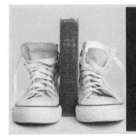

Youth Leader Tip
Don't discount how much influence an opinion from a respected leader can have on your group. Having your church leadership state their faith in front of students encourages their walk with God and will give their faith in God a name and a face.

Read 1 Peter 1:23. God's Word can change us into the kind of people He created us to be. How has the Word of God changed your life?

_____

_____

What area of your life do you want God's Word to change?

_____

_____

Read James 1:22 and Luke 11:28. We are not only supposed to know what God's Word says but also do what it says. Can you think of a time when obeying God's Word saved you from a lot of trouble?

_____

_____

What about a time when disobeying God's Word caused you a lot of trouble?

_____

_____

Read Colossians 3:16-17. Our lives should be saturated in the Word of God so that it even comes out when we are speaking. In your life, what is one way that you can speak God's Word to others?

_____

_____

What is one way you might be able to share God's Word with someone who won't listen?

_____

_____

Read Romans 12:2. Our minds are changed when we renew them through God's Word. With new minds, we can follow God's will more precisely. In what ways has your thinking changed since you started reading the Bible?

_____

_____

Do you have a different perspective about anything? If so, what is it?

_____
_____
_____

Read John 17:17. The only place to find absolute truth is the Bible. What is the most startling truth you've read in the Bible?

_____
_____

Did this truth change you in any way? If so, how?

_____
_____
_____

Read Hebrews 4:12. The Bible can clear up our confusion and help us to make right choices. What are some ways God's Word has directed decisions you have made?

_____
_____

What decisions do you need God's direction to face?

_____
_____
_____

Can you think of what the Bible would say about that situation or what your response should be?

_____
_____

Read Romans 15:4 and 1 Corinthians 10:11. The Bible is full of examples that can encourage and warn us. What story from the Bible has been an encouragement to you? How?

_____
_____

What story from the Bible has warned you? How?

_____
_____
_____

Considering these Scriptures, why would it be important for people to have the Bible available to them to read?

_____
_____

has been waging war against it ever since it was written down. Beginning with book burnings and persecutions under the Roman emperor Nero, the devil has continually stirred up people to try to snuff out the message that God has given to us.[1] Read 1 Peter 1:23-25. Explain that the Word of God, however, is stronger than any attack and will outlast every enemy because it is not just a book. The Bible is filled with the breath—the very life—of God (see 2 Timothy 3:16).

Illustrate this immutability of God's Word by conducting the following object lesson. Hold up the pitcher of water and state that the students have undoubtedly learned about the law of nature (which God created, by the way) called the "conservation of mass." Ask if anyone can remember what that law states. The answer, if no one volunteers, is that matter cannot be created or destroyed in ordinary chemical or physical processes—though it can change from one form to another.

Explain that this law of conservation of mass tells us that if the water in this pitcher is subjected to cold temperatures for a long enough period of time, it will change its form to ice—from a liquid (hold up the pitcher of water) to a solid (hold up the bowl of ice). Ask students if they think that the matter itself was changed. (*The answer is no*—it's still a mass of H_2O molecules stuck together.)

Explain that you will now expose the ice to hot temperatures. When this happens, it will melt and evaporate into a gas called steam (put the water and ice down and use the oven mitt to lift up the tea kettle, which by this time should be steaming). Explain that the matter has changed form again, but it never lost any of its matter. Why? Because it can't. The law of conservation of mass tells us that we cannot destroy matter—we can only cause it to change form. Turn off the burner and place the kettle back on the burner.

Transition to the main point by stating that the Bible has a special conservation law as well. This is not a scientific law but a powerful spiritual truth on which we can depend—in fact, we can bank our futures on it. No matter what forces come against the Word of God, it can never be destroyed. It will continue to exist because it is a product of the very breath of God—eternal life Himself (see 2 Timothy 3:16). The Bible has and will always endure the assault of Satan and unbelieving people because this Book (hold up the Bible) is no ordinary book. It is the living and powerful Word of God.

Have students break into small groups of three to five people. Pass out copies of "Power of the Word" and pens and pencils and have the groups complete the handout. After everyone is finished, regroup and work through each item, discussing each Scripture passage together. Encourage students to expand their concept of the Bible from simply a Christian book to the truth of its life and power as a revelation from their heavenly Father. Conclude by rereading 1 Peter 1:23-25.

DIG

Option 1: Say What? For this option, you will need several Bibles in English (or a language your group members can understand) and a few Bibles in different foreign languages (make sure that at least one is in a language that students will most likely not understand). The American Bible Society has a long list of foreign Bibles that are obtainable at inexpensive prices, or try the library or local bookstore.

Begin by reminding students that we have talked about some of the people that God has used in history to get His Word to us. Now, we will answer this important question: "So what?" Why is it so important that we have the Bible in our own language? To find out, we will listen to a passage of Scripture.

Choose a volunteer to read from the Bible, but hand them one of the foreign language versions—one that you are sure he or she won't be able to read. Ask the volunteer to turn to Psalm 19:7 and to begin to read it aloud. The volunteer should quickly realize that this Bible isn't one they are going to be able to use. When the person objects, tell him or her you're sorry and that you meant to give him or her a different Bible. Hand the person another foreign translation that he or she again will not be able to read. You can play around by passing the Bibles off to different students until the point is clear—the foreign Bibles aren't much benefit unless you can read that language.

Hold up one of the foreign-language Bibles and ask the following questions:

- If you couldn't read the Bible for yourself, how would that affect your walk with God? (*Your understanding of who God is and what He wants for your life would be limited because you would be dependent on someone else to either read it to you or to tell you what's in it.*)
- Why is it dangerous to believe what others tell you is true in the Bible without ever checking it out for yourself? (*Because you could easily be led into error and never know it.*)
- What if I told you that the Bible says only pastors go to heaven? Would you believe it? (*No, because I know the Bible doesn't say that.*)
- But what if you have never read the Bible? (*You would have to either believe or reject what you were told, but you couldn't argue that it's not in there—you couldn't prove it because you haven't read it.*)

Distribute the English Bibles (or a language the students can understand) and have them read Psalm 19:7-11. Discuss the following questions:

- What are some of the characteristics of the Word of God? (*It is perfect, trustworthy, right, radiant, enduring, sure, altogether righteous, precious, pure and sweet.*)
- What are some of the ways that the Bible benefits our lives? (*It revives our souls, makes us wise, gives us joy, gives light, warns us and rewards us.*)

Conclude by asking volunteers to sum up in one sentence why reading the Bible for themselves is so important. In what way does it equip them to fight against the darkness in this world? Try to have each student do this as a way of tying up the point individually.

Option 2: Rusty Treasure. For this option, you will need your Bible and this illustration—although pulling into the room on a Harley would really bring this story to life! Read the following aloud to the group:

There once was a man who collected cars and motorcycles. He bought an old Harley-Davidson for about $600 and stored it in his garage with the idea that he would eventually fix it up and resell it. When he called a motorcycle shop to order some replacement parts, they asked for the bike's ID number. The man gave the information and waited and waited and waited. The clerk from the motorcycle shop came back on the line to verify the numbers. He asked the man to bring the bike into the shop. By now the man was really curious, so he loaded the bike and drove down to the store. When he got there, the clerk and his manager came out to see the bike. Looking it over, they saw a rusty, broken-down motorcycle. Carefully eyeing each part, they lifted the seat and found this inscription: "To Elvis, from James Dean." The man who had purchased the bike was astonished! This old clunker stored away among his garage junk was actually a priceless piece of history that was valued at more than 10 times what he had paid for it! He went home with a whole new appreciation for his unexpected treasure.

Explain that sometimes we don't realize the value of something until someone else points it out to us. Having the Bible available to us in a language we can read is a tremendous gift from God, but sometimes the Bible seems so common that we forget how precious it really is. Read Psalm 19:7-11 and discuss the following:

- What are some of the characteristics of the Word of God? (*It is perfect, trustworthy, right, radiant, enduring, sure, altogether righteous, precious, pure and sweet.*)
- What are some of the ways that the Bible benefits our lives? (*It revives our souls, makes us wise, gives us joy, gives light, warns us and rewards us.*)
- How has this been true in your walk with God? (*Help students tell the ways the Bible has warned, rewarded and guided their own lives. This will emphasize the practicality of daily Bible reading.*)

Conclude by asking volunteers to sum up in one sentence why reading the Bible is important. In what way does it help them to put on the armor of God? Try to have each student do this as a way of tying up the point individually.

APPLY

If you issued the challenge to have students read through the book of Luke in the "A Chapter a Day" option in session 7, they should just about be finished. Check their progress and ask what has impressed them the most from their reading and what they remember the most. Discuss how the Word has become comfortable or familiar to them. What has been the most difficult thing about reading the Bible? Ask if God has revealed Himself to them in a special way. Encourage them to continue until they've finished and trust God to be faithful.

Option 1: Poor Lollard. For this option, you will need lollipops, file-label stickers and a willingness to be contacted by your group members during the week. Ahead of time, write your office phone number or email address on one half of the file labels (either all on the left half or all on the right half). Attach the labels to the stem of the lollipops so that the information is readable.

Explain that back in England after the time of Wycliffe, the poor priests who were the first to take the Word of God to the people in a language they could understand were called Lollards. Tradition has it that they were named this because they talked so much—*la, la, la, la*. . . Ever since that time, we have enjoyed an increasing accessibility to this powerful message from God. The Bible is really God's Word—the sword of the Spirit—and it has much to say to us personally.

Distribute the lollipops and explain that this week, you will be praying specifically for each student that the Word of God will become an anchor to their life and future. You will be asking God to open their spiritual eyes so that they can see His truth and obey it. The lollipop is to remind the students of you—a poor Lollard who can't stop talking about the power of God—who is there to help them discover the powerful, life-changing message of the Bible. If anyone needs an answer to a difficult question or help understanding what they're reading, offer to let them call you. Let them know that you will help them find the answer they need.

Make sure that you have every student's name so that you can pray specifically for him or her. As you do, ask God to give you ways to communicate His truth to those in the group who still aren't persuaded. Write down any Scriptures that come to mind as you pray and be ready to share them with students when you see them during the week. The Word of God is "sharper than any double-edged sword" (Hebrews 4:12), and this is just one way you can show students how effective it can be in their lives.

Option 2: Bookmark Memory Verses 2. This is a continuation of option 2 from session 8. You will need a copy of the "Bookmark Memory Verses" sheet you created at that time. Ahead of time, cut out the bookmark for 1 Peter 1:25.

Begin by giving the group members an opportunity to recite the memory verse from the previous bookmark (2 Timothy 3:16). When they are finished, explain that there is only one thing that will last forever: the Word of God. This is because the Word is an outflow of God Himself—the very breath of God. He will never fade away, and neither will His Word.

Distribute the 1 Peter 1:25 bookmarks and have students read the verse aloud several times. Explain that this memory verse reminds us of the indestructibility of the Word of God. Everything else can and will change, but His Word will not. It is "sharper than any double-edged sword" (Hebrews 4:12) and has the power to cut through the darkness we see around us if we apply it to our lives. God's Word will endure forever.

Before you dismiss the group, remind students of their daily Bible reading challenge. If they haven't been reading at all, encourage them to start today. Close in prayer, asking for God's blessing to draw the student's hearts into a closer fellowship with Himself.

REFLECT

The following short devotions are for the students to reflect on and answer during the week. You can make a copy of these pages and distribute them to your class or download and print them from **www.gospellight.com/uncommon/jh_the_armor_of_god.zip**.

1—HEAR AND OBEY

Who is blessed? Find out in Luke 11:28.

Jesus spoke these words to a crowd that was probably made up of people who were illiterate, which means they couldn't read for themselves. When they went to the synagogue, they heard the Scripture read aloud. Also, back then books were copied totally by hand—the printing press hadn't been invented, so books were expensive and hard to come by. Widespread illiteracy and no printing presses meant that the only way most people had access to God's Word was by listening to it.

If you're reading this, you are literate and can read on your own. Good job! And because of the printing press, the Internet and Bible apps, you can read Scripture any time, anywhere, whether by yourself, with a small group of Christian friends or with your whole youth group or church. Reading is how you "hear" the Word of God.

What's one thing you've heard from God's Word during the last week?

_____

_____

_____

Jesus said we are blessed when we hear *and* obey. How are you doing when it comes to obeying what you've heard?

_____

_____

_____

2—DON'T CONFORM, BE TRANSFORMED

Go your own way to Romans 12:2.

Casey has known his buddies since second grade, and he thought they would always be tight. But lately, Dane, Mack and Freddie really like making fun of people at school, using their humor to bully and tear down pimply or clumsy kids. The four friends used to crack each other up without being mean to people, but now insults seem to be the only humor Casey's buddies know.

This morning when Casey was doing his devotions, he read Mark 12:30-31: "'Love the Lord your God with all your heart and with all your soul and with all your mind and with all your strength' . . . . 'Love your neighbor as yourself.' There is no commandment greater than these."

Later, after fourth period, Casey meets up with his crew in the hall. On the way to lunch, Mack points to Marissa, a chubby sixth-grader, and shouts, "Need help getting to the cafeteria? There's only four of us, but we might be able to roll you down there!" Dane and Freddie bust up laughing, but Casey can't forget the words of Jesus he read before breakfast. If you were Casey, what would you do? (Check all that apply.)

- ❑ Smack Mack on the back of the head and tell him to shut up
- ❑ Keep walking like nothing happened
- ❑ Stop and apologize to Marissa
- ❑ Talk to your friends at lunch about loving their neighbors

How do you think studying God's Word can help you renew your mind and be transformed?

_____

_____

_____

3—ENDURANCE AND HOPE

Test your endurance and check out Romans 15:4.

When the apostle Paul wrote this passage in his letter to the Roman Christians, he was referring to the Old Testament, which is the story of God's faithfulness to His chosen people, the Jews. The events recorded in Genesis through Malachi took place during several thousand years, and they include a lot of ups and downs in the relationship between God and His people.

Think about all of the Bible stories you know. What is a story from the Old Testament that teaches you how to have endurance?

_____

_____

_____

What is a story from the Old Testament that encourages you and gives you hope?

_____

_____

_____

How can the stories in the Old Testament help you stay faithful?

_____

_____

_____

4—DON'T BE A DECEIVER

Do what I say and read James 1:22.

Felicity does "churchy" stuff every chance she gets: worship services twice on Sunday, youth group on Wednesday night, girl's Bible study at lunch on Friday, and youth activities or service projects every other Saturday. She is only 13, but she has already been on five mission trips to other countries. She's also a whiz at memorizing Scripture—she knows all of Psalm 119, the longest chapter in the Bible, by heart and can say all 176 verses super fast in less than two minutes! (You can't really understand what she's saying, but it's still impressive.)

Here's the weird thing about Felicity, though: While she can rattle off all nine fruits of the Spirit (see Galatians 5:22-23), she doesn't seem to have much love, joy, peace, patience, kindness, goodness, faithfulness, gentleness or self-control in her life. She's kind of a know-it-all and a bit of a jerk.

Why is it hard sometimes to put into practice what we learn from God's Word?

_____

_____

_____

What have you read or heard recently from the Bible that you're having a hard time putting into practice?

_____

_____

_____

Say a short prayer asking God's Spirit to give you the strength and discipline you need to do what His Word says.

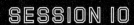

THE BIBLE HAS ONE OVERARCHING MESSAGE

THE BIG IDEA

There are many books that make up the Bible, but it has one overriding message: the redeeming love of God.

SESSION AIMS

In this session, you will guide students to (1) see the unity of the Bible's message; (2) recognize that message to be the redeeming love of God; and (3) respond in gratitude for what He has done for us.

THE BIGGEST VERSE

"The gospel he promised beforehand through his prophets in the Holy Scriptures" (Romans 1:2).

OTHER IMPORTANT VERSES

Genesis 1:27; 2:7; 3:6,8; Psalm 8:4-6; Proverbs 2:1-6; John 3:16-17; 19:30; 20:31; Romans 1:1-2; 5:12,17; 8:21-22; 10:9-10; 12:1-2; Galatians 3:8; Ephesians 1:9-10; 2:10; Colossians 1:13-14; 2:13-14; Titus 2:11-15; Revelation 13:8

Note: Additional options and worksheets in 8¹/₂" x 11" format for this session are available for download at **www.gospellight.com/uncommon/jh_the_armor_of_god.zip**.

STARTER

Option 1: More than a Storybook. For this option, you will need a Bible, five to six storybooks (Aesop's Fables, Grimm's Brothers Fairy Tales, Dr. Seuss stories or any other *collection of stories* grouped around a common theme such as all fables, all fairy tales, and so on), and some students who like to talk. Note that the local library is a good place to pick up a plethora of these books—you can ask the librarian for help and the books are free!

Greet students and have them gather in a circle. Put the storybooks on the floor and let them thumb through them to see if they recognize any of the stories. Begin a discussion by asking the following questions:

- Did you read any of these stories when you were young?
- Have you ever read any of these books to a young child?
- Who read to you when you were younger?
- What was your favorite story?
- What was the first book you remember reading yourself?
- What kinds of books do you like to read now?

Turn to the table of contents in your Bible. Explain that in one way, the Bible is similar to these storybooks. It talks about many different people, places and events that occurred over a long period of history. Ask the group members to name some of their favorite Bible stories. Let them suggest any story they can recollect, and have them tell you which book of the Bible contains that story.

Continue by explaining that the Bible is different from these storybooks for two primary reasons: (1) because it is true, and (2) because it is not just a collection of stories—it is an inspired message of God's redeeming love to us. Ask the group members what it means to "redeem" something? (*To buy it back.*) Explain that from the first book, Genesis, to the last book, Revelation, God has revealed Himself to us as a loving Father who would pay the price needed to buy us back from sin and Satan.

Hold up the Bible with its table of contents visible to the students. State there are 66 books in this revelation, but all of them have only one message. That is what we are going to focus on today: the one message of the Bible.

Option 2: Slinky Races. For this option, you will need your Bible, three Slinkys®, a checkered flag and a long stairway (either indoor or outdoor).

Greet the group members and have them line up against a wall. Count them off into groups of three and have them sit with their groups near the stairway. (This will take some advance thinking, as most stairways are narrow. Be sure to plan it so everyone can see.)

After this, welcome students to the first annual Slinky Race! Explain that this is no ordinary sport. It is a highly skilled, desperately dangerous exercise of physical agility and mental strength. Give each team a Slinky and set the rules for what constitutes a clean race—for example, can the driver give a push if the Slinky gets stuck, or does he or she have to take it to the top and start again? You can also opt to run a few heats and declare the best of two out of three.

Hype this game and encourage wild roars of cheerful enthusiasm from the teams for their Slinky. Have each team select a "driver" who will take the Slinky to the top of the staircase and release it at your signal. When everyone is ready, give a starting signal, wave the flag and watch the race.

After a winning team has been declared, regroup in your meeting room and explain that you know that some of the students might be wondering what a Slinky could possibly have to do with the Bible. State that the Bible itself is like the staircase on which they raced; it is a long, connected pathway. Each step of the staircase is like one book of the Bible. The Slinky is like the message that travels through the pages of this Book. There are many different books (steps), but one message (Slinky).

Explain that there are 66 individual books that make up the whole Bible. Some were written by gray-haired prophets, while others were written by fiery young disciples. The Bible speaks of old men, young men, women, children, wars, romances, famines, invasions, miracles, peasants, kings, and everything in between. There is variety and passion in its pages from Genesis all the way to Revelation. But one message travels through every book, across every page, and that is the message of God's redeeming love. All of the stories in the Bible point toward this theme: God loves us and was willing to pay the price to redeem us.

Explain that the word "redeem" means to buy something or someone back. Through the Bible, God has revealed Himself to us as a loving Father who would pay the price needed to buy us back from sin and Satan. Hold up your Bible and share that there are 66 books in this one revelation, but all of them have only one message. This is what the group is going to discuss during this session.

MESSAGE

Option 1: Book Covers. For this option, you will need several Bibles, a whiteboard, a whiteboard marker and an empty bookcase. In addition, for each small group, you will need eight hard cover books, eight different-colored paper book covers (or pieces of paper large enough to wrap the books, like paper bags), felt-tip pens and a roll of transparent tape. Ahead of time, estimate how many groups of five to eight students will be at the meeting. Set up the whiteboard where all the students can see it, and put the bookcase in the front of the room.

Begin by reminding the students that they have been hearing about some of the great stories and people in the Bible. Today, they will see how everything fits together. There is a thread of unity that connects all the books together—they work as one message from God to us. The Bible is not 66 independent books but a *single* revelation of who God is and what He wants for our lives.

Divide students into small groups of five to eight and have them sit together on the floor. Distribute a Bible, eight books, eight book covers and a roll of transparent tape to each group. Explain that there are two main sections in the Bible: the Old and the New Testament.[1] Write "Old Testament" and "New Testament" on the whiteboard. (Leave some room to write underneath each.)

Have students locate the beginning of the Old Testament and leave it open on the floor in front of them. Explain that the Old Testament includes the people and events that happened before Jesus, centering mostly on the nation of Israel. Now have them locate the beginning of the New Testament and leave it open. Explain that the New Testament includes the life, death and resurrection of Jesus Christ. It also contains about 21 letters to the Church, teaching us how to live for God. Discuss the following questions as a group:

- What are some events recorded in the Old Testament?
- What are some events recorded in the New Testament?

State that these two big sections of the Bible can be broken down into eight smaller sections—four in the Old Testament and four in the New Testament, grouped according to the kind of information that's being recorded. Have the students stack four books on either side of their open Bible.

Now explain that in the Old Testament, they can break the books into these categories: Law, History, Writings and Prophets. Write these four titles on the whiteboard beneath the Old Testament. Instruct each group to cover four of the books you gave them with four different book covers and write a different category title from the board on each one. Under the category title on their books, have the students list the Old Testament books that go in that group. (If your group is familiar with the Bible already, have them try this on their own.)

Once the books are covered, explain that the Law covers the first five books of the Bible, from Genesis through Deuteronomy. Have the students use their Bible's table of contents to find the books and write these names on the book they covered and labeled "Law." As they are writing, explain these are believed to be the oldest books in the Bible. They tell us about creation and the beginning of the Hebrew nation and the laws and commandments God gave to them.

Continue by explaining that the next section, History, covers the things that happened to the nation of Israel from the time they conquered the Promised Land until they were conquered themselves and taken into captivity. These include the books of Joshua through Esther. Have students write these names on their covered book labeled "History."

Next, explain that the third section of the Old Testament, the Writings, are full of songs, prayers, praise, advice on right living, poems of love and philosophical questions about the meaning of life. The Writings include the books of Job through Song of Solomon. Have the students write these names on their covered book labeled "Writings."

Explain that the last section of the Old Testament is the Prophets. These final 17 books, from Isaiah through Malachi, are the words brave men spoke as God moved them to guide His people, Israel, into His will. Have the students write these names on their covered book labeled "Prophets."

State that the Old Testament reveals how much God loves His people. He created a perfect world for them to enjoy, but they rejected Him and were taken captive by sin. Time and time again, God saved them and sent someone—a prophet—to tell them where they went wrong and how to stay out of trouble. But God's people kept turning to their own ways, until eventually they were conquered and taken away as prisoners. But the Bible doesn't end there. Also revealed in the Old Testament is the promise that God would redeem His people and bring them back to His heart again.

Next, you will begin to instruct the students about the second big section in the Bible, the New Testament. This portion tells how God fulfilled the promise to redeem and bring back His people through the life, death and resurrection of His Son, Jesus Christ. Have students wrap the next stack of books with the remaining book covers. Explain that the New Testament can also be divided into four smaller sections: the Gospels, History, Letters and Prophecy. Have students label the books with these four titles.

State that the Gospels are made up of four books: Matthew, Mark, Luke and John. Each of these tells about Jesus' life on earth and what He did to save us. Have students write these names on their covered book labeled "Gospels."

Explain that the second section, History, has only one book: Acts. This book tells how the first Church spread the news of Jesus all over their world. Have students write this name on their covered book labeled "History."

Continue by stating that the next section of the New Testament, the Letters, are literally that—*letters*. There are 21 of them to be exact, written by the apostles. They start with the book of Romans and end with the book of Jude. They are about how to live for God, how to treat each other in a way that honors Him, and how Jesus' work on the cross should touch our lives. Have students write these names on their covered book labeled "Letters."

State that the last section of the New Testament, Prophecy, is also only one book: Revelation. This book is the record of a vision God gave to John about what would happen before Jesus comes back again. Have students write this name on their covered book labeled "Prophecy."

Now have the group members mix up their eight books and see if they can put them into the right biblical order. Give each member a chance to do it at least once. When everyone is done, have the groups arrange their books in right Bible order on the bookshelf in the front of the room. Read John 20:31 and explain these books were written so we can believe in Jesus and what He has done for us. The message of the Bible is the redeeming love of God. All the individual books relate to God's plan to buy us back from the power of sin. Throughout the Bible, God reveals Himself to us as a loving Father who is willing to pay the price to free us and bring us back into a close relationship with Himself.

Option 2: A Bird's-Eye View of the Bible. For this option, you will need several Bibles, copies of "A Bird's-Eye View of the Bible" (found on the next page), a copy of the leader reference guide (included in the worksheet files available for download), maps of different states and an aerial picture or satellite photo of the United States. You can locate these through travel and map companies, or bring in a laptop, find these on Google and show them to the students. Begin this option by discussing the following questions:

- How does a person's viewpoint of something affect how he or she perceives things? (*A person's viewpoint can cause that person to miss some things and single out others. For example, if you were standing next to an elephant, you might describe it as a "gray, wrinkly, rough wall." If you were standing 20 feet away, you would describe it as a large animal with a trunk, tusks and large ears.*)

- What do we mean when we say someone has a bird's-eye view? (*That he or she is "looking down" on something or has a wide view, such as the person who is standing 20 feet away from the elephant. The person is seeing the thing as a whole and is not limited to ground-level viewing.*)

A Bird's-Eye View of the Bible

What's in It?

1. _____
2. _____
3. _____
4. _____
5. _____
6. _____
7. _____
8. _____
9. _____
10. _____

How to Find It

1. Two main sections: The _____ _____ and _____ _____.
2. The Old Testament includes events _____ Jesus and center mostly on the nation of _____.
3. The New Testament includes the _____, _____, and _____ of Jesus Christ. It also contains __ letters to believers, teaching us how to _____ for God.
4. The table of contents in my Bible is on page _____.

Where to Find It

1. If I wanted to read about creation, where would I look? _____
2. If I wanted to read about Jesus' miracles, where would I look? _____
3. If I wanted to read about King David, where would I look? _____
4. If I wanted to read about the apostles' teaching, where would I look? _____
5. What are some other events recorded in the Old Testament? _____
   _____
   _____

6. What are some other events recorded in the New Testament? _____
   _____
   _____

How It Fits Together

1. The one message of the Bible is _____ _____ _____ ___ _____. All the books re-late to God's plan to buy us back from the power of _____.
2. Write out John 20:31: _____
   _____

3. Have you received the gift this verse is talking about? Why or why not? _____
   _____
   _____

- What are the benefits of having a bird's-eye view? (*You get a better idea of how the pieces relate to each other so you understand it better.*)

Open up some of the state maps and lay them out where students can see. (If you are using the laptop option, show the maps you found on Google.) Explain that these maps tell us about a small part of our country. By looking at them, we can see generally how to get around, but we don't really know what each state has to do with the other or how they are related.

Now show the aerial picture of the country. Explain that by looking at this picture, we can get a better idea of how each of these smaller pieces fit together. If we didn't have this bird's-eye view, we might never realize that these states work together and form one landmass we call the United States. Ask the group what they think it means to have a bird's-eye view of the Bible. (*The answer would be that it is to see how each book of the Bible is an important part of understanding the one, common message of the Bible.*) Continue by stating that the Bible's one overriding message is God's redeeming love for us. We can better see how this single message is in each book by realizing how all of the books fit together and how they are related to each other. Each one gives us further understanding into God's great love and His plan to redeem us from sin.

Distribute "A Bird's-Eye View of the Bible" and pens or pencils. Explain that if we want to have a bird's-eye view of God's revelation in the Bible, we need to know the general pieces with which we are working. To this end, you will be taking the students through the major happenings in the Bible and putting together a sequence of events. Go through each of the sections using the leader reference guide in the worksheet files available for download.

In the "what's in it?" section, ask the questions on the leader's guide and have the students write down a brief summary in the numbered blanks. The goal is to help students see the flow of major events and people in the Bible. Help students see the logical order to the events you discuss by asking how each connects to the one next to it. Given this bird's-eye view, how do these events, and the books that record these events, relate to each other?

The second section, "how to find it," helps students know where to look to find these events. Have them fill in the blanks as you go along. Once the group members have filled in these blanks, have them draw a line between numbers 6 and 7 in the "what's in it?" section. This will show which events are found in the Old Testament and which are found in the New Testament.

Discuss the questions in the "where to find it" section on the handout. State that the basic sequence of what is in the Bible and where to find those events helps us understand how they fit together. Beginning in Genesis, we see God's desire to have a close relationship with us. He made Adam and Eve in His image for that reason. When they sinned, God's ideal world was broken, but this did not surprise Him. He knew when He created Adam that He would also need to provide a way to salvation not only for him but also for all humankind. Read Romans 1:1-2, Galatians 3:8 and Revelation 13:8. Discuss the following:

- What does the "gospel he promised beforehand" mean (Romans 1:1-2)? (*That the Old Testament is really a giant arrow pointing to Christ's coming as our savior and deliverer.*)
- How does Galatians 3:8 echo this idea? (*Let students reread the verse and explain it in their own words.*)
- When was Jesus, our perfect Passover Lamb, slain (see Revelation 13:8)? (*Before the world was created. In other words, God had already provided a way of deliverance for us.*)
- What do these verses say about the plan of God? (*That God's plan was already in place before the world was created. He was and is in control of everything. All the books of the Bible point toward this.*)

Conclude by having the group members fills out the "how it fits together" section on their own (the blanks for question 1 are "the redeeming love of God" and "sin"). Reiterate that the one message of the Bible is the redeeming love of God and that all of the books relate to God's plan to buy us back from the power of sin. God reveals Himself to us as a loving Father who was willing to pay the price to free us and bring us back into close relationship with Himself.

DIG

Option 1: Spiritual Treasure. For this option, you will need several Bibles, a five-foot diameter plastic pool, sand, 75 to 100 coins (a mixture of pennies, nickels, dimes, quarters, coin dollars), chocolate candy coins and a vacuum. Ahead of time, place the plastic pool in a place where the students can get around it. Put the coins in the pool and cover them with sand.

Invite eight students to come to the pool of sand and divide them into two teams of four. At your signal, the teams will dig through the sand to find whatever they can. (If they don't trust you, explain that there's nothing gross in the sand—honest!) After two minutes, signal a stop and have the teams count their change. The losing team can vacuum up any spilled sand. Applaud the winning team and begin a discussion by asking the volunteers the following questions:

- How did you feel when I asked you to dig? (*Unsure of what to expect.*)
- After you found a few coins, how did your expectations change? (*I got excited and dug faster in hopes of finding more.*)
- How did the value of the coin affect the effort you invested? (*The more we value something, the more effort we're willing to put into it.*)
- What if you dug and found used gym socks? (*I'd probably stop.*)
- What if you had found a $100 bill? (*I'd probably search the pool dry!*)
- How is reading the Bible like digging for treasure? (*It takes a little work and sometimes we don't know what to expect, but if we are willing to make an effort, we will find a huge wealth of the knowledge about God.*)

Distribute Bibles and have a volunteer read Proverbs 2:1-6. Explain that the Word of God is like this pool filled with sand. The sand is full of hidden treasure just waiting for us to dig out. As we read the Word, the Holy Spirit works in our hearts to bring understanding and insight that can revolutionize our lives. But we have to dig. As we begin to understand how the parts of the Bible fit together to communicate God's message to us, we start to realize just how powerful and meaningful the Scriptures really are. Discuss the following questions:

- What are the responsibilities of the seeker? (*To accept, store up, turn an ear to, apply the heart to, call out, cry aloud, look for, and search for God's Word [Proverbs 2:1-4].*)
- What are the rewards of the seeker? (*Understanding, knowledge and wisdom [verses 5-6].*)

Conclude by sharing that the Bible is full of God's message of redeeming love—love that reaches out to us daily! Hold up your Bible and state that when we open this book, we can expect God to give us spiritual treasure that will enrich our walk with Him. That's why He gave the Bible to us in the first place—so we could know Him better. Give each student a chocolate coin to remind them of the treasure hidden in the Word.

Option 2: Comstock Lode. For this option, you will need this true story. Read the following to the group members:

It was late in 1857 when a man bought a mine in western Nevada in hopes of discovering gold. He had used all his money to buy the mine and spent nearly every waking hour of the next two years inside that mine digging. He didn't find very much at first, a small nugget here and there, but it was enough for him to afford to buy food and supplies and keep on digging.

Day after day the man was there, chipping away at the stone with his rusty pickax. Soon he became discouraged. One day in frustration, he picked up his ax, swung it back over his head, and with one blow completely imbedded the ax in the side of a rock wall. Then he took his lantern, walked out of the mine, and headed straight into town. He sold the mine on the spot for far less than he had bought it two years ago.

The man who purchased the mine was named H. T. Comstock. After he bought it, he took his wheelbarrow, his lantern and mining tools and marched up to the mountain to check it out. He lit the lantern to survey the stone walls and came across the pickax stuck deep into the side of the wall. Comstock wondered about the imbedded pickax. He decided that it still looked useful, so he proceeded to push and pull until he got the other man's pickax out of the wall.

When he did, a large portion of rock and dirt crumbled to the ground, revealing the single largest find of gold and silver in the western United States. It became known as the Comstock Lode.

Sum up by stating that sometimes we are tempted to give up when we don't see the immediate value of something. Reading the Bible is like digging for gold. There is some effort that goes into it, and sometimes it can seem like a lot of work and no payoff. But God rewards diligent seekers. If we continue to have a regular time of Bible reading, we will hit a "mother lode" of revelation and truth. The Holy Spirit is waiting to open our eyes to the love of God revealed in His Word. We just have to keep swinging!

Read Proverbs 2:1-6. Explain that this verse tells us the Word of God is full of treasure. It is there. The real question is, are we willing to dig for it? Conclude by stating that the Bible is full of God's message of redeeming love—love that reaches out to each one of us every day! When we open this book, we can expect God to give us spiritual treasure that will enrich our walk with Him. That's why He gave the Bible to us in the first place—so we could know Him better.

APPLY

Option 1: Nailing Sin to the Cross. For this option, you will need a large wooden cross, paper, a felt-tip pen, a hammer and a nail. Ahead of time, write the word "sin" in big letters on the paper.

Read Colossians 2:13-14 and ask the group members if they have ever had to bring a bad report card home. Explain that this is how they can understand what it's like to have their failures written down, ready to accuse them in front of everyone. In reality, their sins were written down and were ready to accuse them as well. However, Jesus took that list of sins and nailed it to the cross, where it was destroyed. Nail the paper to the cross.

Explain that we no longer stand accused if we have received the grace and forgiveness of God by believing in Jesus. Ask the students if they have accepted the love of God and His gift of new life. Lead students in a time of prayer, specifically focusing on those who have yet to receive Christ. Lead them as the Holy Spirit directs you, but don't let them leave without having a chance to accept Jesus into their hearts. Make yourself available afterward to talk about their decision, and contact them during the week to check in and answer any questions that arise. Close with a final prayer thanking God for His one message of amazing, redeeming love.

Option 2: Bookmark Memory Verses 3. This is a continuation of option 2 from sessions 8 and 9. You will need a copy of the "Bookmark Memory Verses" sheet you previously created. Ahead of time, cut out the bookmark for John 20:31.

Begin by giving the group members an opportunity to recite the memory verse from the previous bookmark (1 Peter 1:25). When they are finished, distribute the John 20:31 bookmark and have them read the verse aloud several times. Explain that this session's memory verse tells us the reason God had people write down His Word: so that we would believe in Jesus and receive eternal life.

Explain that as they think about this verse, they should consider how it reminds them of the one message of the Bible. Before you dismiss the group, remind students of their daily Bible reading challenge. If they haven't been reading at all, encourage them to start today. Close in prayer, asking for God's blessing and grace to work in the lives of your students.

Youth Leader Tip

The more familiar you make the Bible to your students, the more likely they will be to see its value. By telling them what's inside, how to find it and how it fits together, you are giving them a priceless framework for their ongoing study of God's Word.

REFLECT

The following short devotions are for the students to reflect on and answer during the week. You can make a copy of these pages and distribute them to your class or download and print them from **www.gospellight.com/uncommon/jh_ the_armor_of_god.zip**.

1—STUDENTS OF GRACE

What does grace teach you? Find out in Titus 2:11-14.

Grace is an excellent teacher, as Riley will tell you. Her favorite subject in school has always been history, but this year it's tough because the teacher, Mr. Jacobsen, seems more interested in beating the school record for detentions than in helping his students learn anything. Riley's teachers have always given her good marks for hard work and class participation, but Mr. Jacobsen calls raising your hand to ask a question "interrupting." The worst part is that Riley has never been a great speller, and even when she gets the test answers correct, Mr. Jacobsen counts them wrong if they are misspelled. In her favorite subject, she's barely scraping by with a C–!

But science, Riley's least favorite subject, is a different story. Her teacher, Mrs. Palmer, eats lunch in her classroom every day to study with kids who need extra help remembering the difference between earth's crust, mantle and core. Mrs. Palmer reminds her students, "There's no such thing as a stupid question," and even gives out a prize if someone asks her a question for which she doesn't know the answer—and then the whole class researches the answer together. Riley never knew science was so much fun, and she's giving serious consideration to making it her new favorite subject.

Mrs. Palmer is a better teacher for Riley than Mr. Jacobsen because (check all that apply):

- ❑ She goes out of her way to help her students learn
- ❑ She knows all the answers to every question
- ❑ She makes it okay to make mistakes because it's a part of learning

What does Titus 2:11-14 tell us that God's grace teaches us?

_____

_____

_____

Living godly lives is a hard subject, even more than science. Why do you think God's grace is a good teacher for something that's so hard to learn?

_____

_____

_____

2—JESUS AND THE WORD

Galatians 5:8 is pretty amazing, but you should see for yourself.

The Bible is a miracle! You have several thousand years of history before Jesus came, recorded in the Old Testament, and then Jesus and the beginnings of the Church in the New Testament. (All the New Testament events took place in less than 100 years.) After Jesus ascended into heaven, His first followers noticed something as they re-read the Old Testament Scriptures they had grown up with: A lot of them were about Christ, even though they had been written hundreds of years before He came! In fact, as the first Christians applied what they knew about Jesus to God's Word, the Old Testament began to make sense in a way that it hadn't ever before.

Read Isaiah 53:3-5. This is one of the Old Testament passages the early Christians could see Jesus in. Why do you think they recognized Jesus in these words?

_____

_____

_____

Abraham is the "founding father" of the Jewish people. The earliest Christians understood God's promise to Abraham that all nations would be blessed through him to mean Jesus. Why do you think that is?

_____

_____

_____

Write a short prayer thanking God for the crazy miracle of His Word and for the blessing of salvation through Christ!

_____

_____

_____

3—LOVE LETTER

You're on God's mind, according to Psalm 8:4-6.

Justin isn't very good in school, and he's terrible at sports. He can't carry a tune to save his life, and the one time he tried out for the school play, his voice cracked during the audition—so embarrassing! He's got two older brothers and a younger sister who are all good at something, and a grandma who always calls him by someone else's name. Basically, Justin feels like a nobody, and it's easy to understand why.

Do you think today's verse might encourage Justin? Why or why not?

_____
_____
_____
_____

Do you believe that God made you "a little lower than the angels" and that you are crowned "with glory and honor"? Why or why not?

_____
_____
_____
_____

How does it feel to know that God is thinking of you?

_____
_____
_____
_____
_____

4—GOD'S WILL

Get in the know by reading Ephesians 1:9-10.

Ever wonder what God's will is? Well, wonder no longer! The apostle Paul says in this verse that God's will is "to bring unity to all things in heaven and on earth under Christ." No more conflict, no more fighting, no more wars—peace forever under Christ's reign. Can you imagine?

It's great to know where we're headed and what we can expect, but how do we know what to do in the meantime? That's what the rest of Scripture is for! How does the Bible reveal God's will to us?

_____

_____

_____

_____

How does the Bible let us know how God feels about us?

_____

_____

_____

_____

Why is it so important to make Bible reading a part of your daily life?

_____

_____

_____

_____

If you haven't already made a plan to spend time in God's Word each day, do it today!

THE BIBLE HAS ONE OVERRIDING STORY

THE BIG IDEA

There are many people, places and events depicted in the Bible, but it has one central story: the story of Jesus Christ.

SESSION AIMS

In this session, you will guide students to (1) see that the Old Testament points forward to Jesus; (2) understand that His coming means our freedom and salvation; and (3) read the Bible with a better grasp of God's plan and a deeper sense of gratefulness for what He has done.

THE BIGGEST VERSE

"And beginning with Moses and all the Prophets, he explained to them what was said in all the Scriptures concerning himself" (Luke 24:27).

OTHER IMPORTANT VERSES

Isaiah 53:5; Micah 5:2; Zechariah 12:10; Matthew 4:4; 16:21; Luke 24:44; John 20:31; 1 Corinthians 2:12; 15:3-4

Note: Additional options and worksheets in 8¹/₂" x 11" format for this session are available for download at **www.gospellight.com/uncommon/jh_the_armor_of_god.zip**.

STARTER

Option 1: Arrow Course. For this option, you will need your Bible, paper in three different colors (12 to 15 sheets each), scissors, masking tape, a timer and prizes. Ahead of time, cut arrows out of the paper. Mark out three different courses through the buildings and open areas of your church. Tape the arrows (by color) to walls, poles, the ground as guides to get through each course. (*Note:* The group members will be running the courses, collecting the arrows, and racing to get back to the meeting room. You might want to alert anyone else in the building of what is going on so that they aren't wondering why junior-highers are taking over the premises.)

Greet the group members and welcome them back to this study on the Word of God, our weapon in our spiritual arsenal to combat the darkness in this world. Bring those who are new up to speed by asking others to share some of the things they have learned during the past few weeks. If there is a long silent pause and lots of blank stares, try prompting them with a few questions about the uniqueness of the Bible, its reliability and its indestructibility. Ask them to share something from their personal Bible reading. If they still have no idea what you're talking about, then check the room number on the door—maybe you're in the wrong place.

Begin by telling the group members that today they will be going on a speed mission. Choose three students to act as team leaders, and then count off the rest of the students by threes so you end up with three fairly equal teams. Assign each team one of the three colors of arrows and explain that when you give the signal, each team must lock arms and follow a course marked by their colored arrow. When a team gets to an arrow, they must pull it down and bring it with them while they collect all of their colored arrows. Each team must collect a specified number of arrows (give them an exact number depending on what you put out there) and then return to the room before the timer goes off to win the prize. Remind everyone in the group to keep their arms locked!

Set the timer for five minutes. (If you know that your students will need more time because of your location, set the timer for a longer period.) Signal the start, and have a cup of coffee. Just kidding! You and other adult leaders can accompany a group or go out and supervise the controlled chaos. When everyone is back, award prizes to those teams who kept their arms locked, retrieved all their colored arrows, and were back before the timer went off. Explain that the arrows remind us that often things are not an end in and of themselves. They are pieces that point to something else.

Hold up your Bible and remind students that they have learned a lot about the Word of God these past few weeks. Last session, the group focused on the idea that the Bible has one overriding message—the redeeming love of God. In today's session, we are going to hone in on this truth and discuss how the Bible has one overriding story—the story of Jesus Christ. Everything in God's Word points to Him.

Option 2: Unroll the Poster. For this option, you will need your Bible, five posters of familiar people or scenes (such as famous sports or entertainment people, wildlife, recognizable places like Hawaii or Alaska), rubber bands, push-pins and prizes. Ahead of time, roll the posters with the picture inside and secure it with a rubber band.

Greet your group once again and ask about their week. See if anyone would like to share something from his or her personal Bible reading. Also ask the group how they have used the Bible this week as a "sword" to overcome a temptation or help them choose to do the right thing. Don't rush this, because while some students will be dying to talk, others will need time to work up some courage. When everyone has had a chance to share, divide the students into two teams and have them sit together facing the front of the room. Explain that you will be slowly unrolling a poster two inches at a time. After each unrolling, each team will get one guess as to what the whole picture is. Teams can discuss ideas together, but you must accept the first answer they give you.

The best way to do the unrolling is to pin up the two top corners of the poster to a wall facing the students. (You can have an adult helper do this for you and you can just emcee the process instead.) Carefully unroll the poster two inches at a time and have students make their guesses. Award 1,000 points to the team who first guesses correctly. When the picture has been correctly identified, unroll it all the way and pin the bottom to the wall. Repeat the process with each of the posters.

Give prizes to the winning team and continue by reminding students that they have been learning a lot about the Bible during these past sessions—what's in it and why it's reliable. Today, you want the group to focus on the one overriding story of the Bible: the story of Jesus Christ. Hold up your Bible and state that just as you unrolled the posters a little at a time until they got enough of the picture to understand what it was, the Bible paints a picture, beginning with Genesis 1:1, of Jesus and His story. As we read through each book of the Bible, it carefully reveals more and more of who He is and what He has done to buy our redemption.

MESSAGE

Option 1: Road to Emmaus. For this option, you will need several Bibles, three Bible-times costumes (tunics or bathrobes, head coverings, walking sticks, sandals, leather money pouch, and so on), four volunteers (either students or adults), a basket of bread, a table and several loaves of bread. Ahead of time, have the volunteers practice acting out Luke 24:13-32. Two of them will portray the men on their way from Jerusalem to Emmaus, one will portray Jesus, and one will be a narrator. As much as possible, use the Bible text itself as dialogue. Clear a path down the center of the room for the volunteers to use as a road to Emmaus. Set up the table at the front of the meeting room and place the basket of bread on it.

Begin by reminding students that we previously discussed that the overriding message of the Bible is the redeeming love of God. This week, we are going to learn what the one overriding *story* of the Bible is: Jesus Christ and His promise of eternal life. Both the Old and New Testaments point to the story of Jesus. The Bible unfolds a picture of Him beginning in Genesis and continuing all the way through Revelation.

Have the volunteers act out the passage from Luke 24:13-32. They should move from the back of the room to the front and end up sitting at the table up front to eat the bread. To show Jesus disappearing (see verse 31), you will need to have a way that the volunteer can duck behind something. Don't worry if it's not realistic. Students will likely laugh and understand!

After the skit, have the group members move to the different parts of the room where the story was acted out—either at the beginning of the "road," on the way at the middle of the road, or where they ate dinner at the end of the road. Explain that you are going to ask them questions pertaining to that part of the story. Ask the students at the beginning of the road the following:

- From where were the two men coming? (*Jerusalem.*)
- Where were they going? (*To Emmaus, about seven miles away.*)
- What were they doing as they walked? (*Talking about the things that had happened recently in Jerusalem.*)

Ask the students who moved to the middle of the road the following:

- Who joined up with the two men? (*Jesus.*)
- Did they recognize Him? (*No.*)
- What did Jesus ask them? (*He asked what they were talking about.*)

- What was their response? (*They thought Jesus was from a different country because He hadn't heard about all that was happening in the city.*)
- What did they tell Jesus? (*They told Him about the life, death and resurrection of Jesus [kind of weird, huh?].*)
- Did they understand what had happened? (*No, they were confused.*)
- What was Jesus' response? (*He explained how all the Scriptures from Moses to the Prophets had spoken about this event. It was already written down for all to see. He then started at the beginning and explained it all to them—how the story of Jesus was found even in the Old Testament.*)

Ask the students at the front of the room, near the table, the following:

- What time of day was it when the men arrived at Emmaus? (*Dinnertime.*)
- What did the men ask of Jesus? (*If He would have a meal with them.*)
- What did they eat? (*Bread.*)
- Who blessed the meal? (*Jesus prayed over it. Then He took the bread from the meal, broke it and gave it to them.*)
- What happened when Jesus gave them the bread? (*Their eyes were opened and they recognized who He really was.*)
- How did Jesus leave the men? (*He disappeared.*)
- What was the men's reaction to Jesus' teaching? (*Their hearts "burned within them." They finally understood what they had read in their Bible for years—that the whole message of the Bible points to the story of Jesus and the promise He gives of forgiveness and salvation.*)

Have the group members return to their seats. Explain that there is a difference between knowing something as a fact and knowing something as a reality. Although the two journeying men had learned all their lives about the Bible and had possibly even witnessed Jesus' death, it wasn't until Jesus Himself broke the bread and gave it to them that the reality of those words came to life.[1] Distribute a slice of bread to each student. State that throughout the Bible, bread is used to symbolize the Word of God. Just as we all need to eat food to live physically, we need to eat spiritual food to live spiritually.

Have volunteers read Deuteronomy 8:3, Matthew 4:4 and John 6:32-35. Explain that Jesus said He was the Bread of Life and that by receiving Him, we could have eternal life. Jesus is the way to life. By His death and resurrection, we can be forgiven of sin and made a part of God's family. Jesus made a way for redeeming love to touch our lives and bring us into His family forever.

Option 2: It's All About You, Jesus. For this option, you will need several Bibles, copies of "It's All About You, Jesus" (found on the next page), pens or pencils, a walking stick, a phone (it doesn't have to work), and a pair of glasses. Distribute Bibles and have students turn to Luke 24:13. Assign the verses evenly among your group members so that each person reads at least one verse. Distribute copies of "It's All About You, Jesus" and pens or pencils. Have students fill in the blanks as you explain the following points.

Under the first section, "the Road to Emmaus," explain that Jesus met the men on the <u>road</u>, and He meets <u>us</u> where we are as well. Hold up the walking stick and state that like these two men, all of us are on a journey—a journey of life. Along that walk, Jesus comes to us and meets us right where we are. No matter where we are on our journey—whether we are seeking Christ or are believers in Christ—Jesus wants to walk with us and direct our steps.

Next, explain that Jesus was <u>interested</u> in what the men were talking about, and He is interested in <u>our</u> <u>lives</u> as well. The men who were making the journey in this story had just come from Jerusalem, where a Jewish prophet named Jesus had been arrested and crucified. These two men had just seen the most promising prophet in Israel—the one they perhaps thought would lead the nation of Israel to freedom from the Romans—killed on a cross and then vanish from His tomb. They had a lot to talk about!

Explain that the men were confused and were discussing the event in an attempt to make some sense of it. Jesus not only met them along the road but also was interested in what was important to them. Hold up the phone and state that Jesus cares about the things we are dealing with as well. Talking with Him about the things that are going on in our lives invites His presence to work in those things and bring about His perfect will.

Next, explain that Jesus cleared up their <u>confusion</u>, just as He <u>opens</u> <u>our</u> <u>eyes</u> to the truth. These two men had probably been raised in Jewish homes all their lives. They knew what their Bible, the Old Testament, said and were well acquainted with its teachings and traditions. However, they still didn't "get" it. Although they had talked about everything that had happened, they couldn't see that the Scriptures had foretold everything that had transpired. They didn't see that the Bible was much more than the story of their people, the Jews—it actually revealed God's heart of love to redeem His people from sin.

Continue by stating that the Scriptures were written so that we can know God and understand His plan. God's love touches our lives through His Son, Jesus Christ. Like these men, we can know a lot about the Bible but still miss the point. We need Jesus to help it make sense to us. Hold up the glasses and explain

It's All About You, Jesus

The Road to Emmaus (Luke 24:13-32)

1. Jesus met the men on the _____, and He meets _____ where we are at as well (verses 13-16).

2. Jesus was _____ in what the men talking about, and He is interested in ____ _____ as well (verses 17-24).

3. Jesus cleared up their _____, just as He _____ ____ _____ to the truth (verses 25-32).

The Scriptures Speak of Jesus

Look up the following verses and write down what they say about how the Old Testament points to the story of Jesus.

Scripture	What does this say about how the Old Testament points to Jesus?
John 5:39,46	
Luke 24:44-47	
Acts 3:18	
Acts 17:2-3	
1 Corinthians 15:3-4	

that this is what Jesus does—He puts the "glasses" on our eyes so we can see clearly. Have the group members look up the Scriptures under "the Scriptures Speak of Jesus" section and indicate how these verses point to Jesus.

Conclude by stating that the signs of Jesus' coming and His death and resurrection were all throughout the Old Testament. From start to finish, the Bible is truly the story of Jesus Christ.

DIG

Option 1: It's All About Jesus. For this option, you will need several Bibles, index cards, a pen, a basket and some junior-high Bible scholars. Ahead of time, write the following Bible references and corresponding question on an index card (note that some of the same Bible references are used twice). Fold the card in half and put it in the basket. (The answers to each question are included in parentheses for your easy reference.)

- John 5:39: Who do the Scriptures speak of? (*Jesus.*)
- John 5:46: Who did Moses write about? (*Jesus.*)
- John 5:46: What part of the Bible does "Moses" refer to? (*The Books of the Law—Genesis through Deuteronomy.*)
- Luke 24:44: What part of the Bible does the "Law of Moses," "the Prophets" and "the Psalms" refer to? (*The Law of Moses, the Prophets and the Psalms—basically, the entire Old Testament.*)
- Luke 24:46: What events were written in the Old Testament about Jesus? (*His suffering, death and resurrection.*)
- Acts 3:18: Who fulfilled what had been foretold? What was foretold? (*God fulfilled what the prophets had foretold. The fact that Christ would suffer was foretold.*)
- Acts 17:2-3: Who went to the synagogue? What did he do there? (*Paul went to the synagogue and reasoned with the Jews from the Scriptures.*)
- Acts 17:2-3: What did Paul explain from the Scriptures? Who did he say was this Christ? (*Paul explained that the Christ had to suffer and rise from the dead. This was Jesus.*)
- 1 Corinthians 15:3-4: Christ died according to what? ("According" means it happened just the way it was said.) (*Christ died according to the Scriptures, which meant the Old Testament, because the New Testament had not been written yet.*)
- 1 Corinthians 15:3-4: What events are referred to in the Scriptures? (*Jesus' burial and resurrection.*)

Explain that at first, it might seem a little strange to say that the Old Testament is really all about Jesus. After all, His name isn't even mentioned once! Can we really say that the whole Bible is the story of Jesus? Distribute Bibles and have students take turns drawing a card and reading the Scripture reference for everyone to look up. As a group, answer the question that goes with each verse.

Read Matthew 16:21 and explain that Jesus used the Old Testament to tell His disciples what was going to happen to Him. Choose two volunteers to read the Bible verses list below. Assign the first volunteer only the Old Testament verses and the second volunteer only the New Testament verses. Reading the verses one right after the other will help to highlight the distinct promise given in the Old Testament and how it was fulfilled in the New Testament.

Prophecy	Old Testament	New Testament
Jesus' arrival on earth	Micah 5:2	Matthew 2:6
Jesus' death on the cross	Jonah 1:17	Matthew 12:40
	Psalm 22:1	Matthew 27:46
	Isaiah 53:5	John 19:34
	Zechariah 12:10	John 19:37
Jesus' victory as King and Deliverer	Psalm 22:22	Hebrews 2:12
	Hosea 13:14	1 Corinthians 15:55,57

Conclude by stating that there are at least 60 major prophecies in the Old Testament about the Messiah, and not just one or two but all of those prophecies were fulfilled through Jesus Christ. Jesus continually reminded His disciples, "These things were written . . ." referring to the Old Testament. The events in His life happened in accordance with God's plan.

Option 2: Jacob's Story. For this option, you will just need this story. Read the following aloud to the group:

Jacob's grandparents were from Russia and had immigrated to America in the early 1900s. They and his parents were committed Jews who took every opportunity they could to maintain a sense of Jewish identity in their new country. Jacob had grown up hearing the stories of Abraham, Isaac and his namesake, Jacob. He knew all about the conquering of the Promised Land and King David. He could quote long segments of the Old Testament by heart in Hebrew. He attended synagogue every week and enjoyed his rich heritage of faith. His family was proud of him and had high hopes for him.

One day at lunch, Jacob sat next to a girl named Karen. She was in his algebra class, but the two hadn't talked much. Karen said hello when Jacob sat down, and then bowed her head. Jacob could see her lips moving, but barely a whisper came out.

"What are you doing?" Jacob asked.

"Oh, just thanking God for my lunch," Karen replied.

"Really?" said Jacob. "Are you Jewish?"

"No, I'm a Christian," answered Karen.

"Oh." Jacob thought for a minute. *A Christian? Too bad. She was kind of cute.*

"You know," Karen continued, "Christianity came from Judaism. In fact, Jesus was a Jew. We believe that the Jewish Scriptures are God's Word and that they pointed the way to the coming of the Messiah, Jesus Christ."

Jacob shuddered at the thought. In his mind, Jews were Jews and Christians were Christians—they were not the same. And to say that the Old Testament spoke about Jesus as the Messiah—no way!

Jacob set down his apple. "Well, you're wrong," he said. "The Law and Prophets talk about Jewish history, not about Jesus. His name is not even mentioned once!"

"He might not be mentioned by name," said Karen, "but His message and story are on every page."

Conclude by having volunteers read the following Scriptures: John 5:39,46; Luke 24:44-47; Acts 3:18; 17:2-3; and 1 Corinthians 15:3-4. As the volunteers read, discuss how each passage might be helpful in speaking with someone like Jacob. Try to dig out what parts of the Scriptures speak of Jesus and what specific events the Scriptures foretell.

APPLY

Option 1: Light of Understanding. For this option, you will need fireplace matches (with the lid to light them), several candles in candleholders, and an adult helper. Ahead of time, set up the candles around the room, being careful to place them where they can't get knocked over or catch anything on fire. (Note: Always have a fire extinguisher ready when using matches!)

Begin by sharing that just like those men on the road to Emmaus, we need God to open our eyes to see the truth. Dim the room lights and light a single match. Explain that when Jesus taught the men on the Emmaus road, He started at the beginning and explained God's whole plan of salvation. Afterward, the Bible says that the men's eyes "were opened and they recognized him" (Luke 24:31).

Explain that you want to start at the beginning as well by saying that God loves each of them and wants to bring them into His family. The way has been made and Jesus is standing at the door, just waiting for them to enter (see Revelation 3:20). Ask if anyone who has not done so would like to receive this gift of salvation offered through the life, death and resurrection of Jesus Christ. Will they let Him spark a life-changing flame in their lives right now? Will they let Him open their eyes? Have an adult helper use the remaining matches to light the candles. Be sure there are enough to give adequate light to move around the room. If not, turn back on a few of the lights.

Continue to appeal to the group as the Holy Spirit directs. Believe that the Lord will move in the hearts of students who have yet to receive Christ and that God can—and will—draw even the hardest hearts to Himself. Close with a prayer of blessing over the students, asking God to enrich their walk with Him through new insights into His Word.

Option 2: Bookmark Memory Verses 4. This is a continuation of option 2 from sessions 8–10. You will need a copy of the "Bookmark Memory Verses" sheet you created at that time. Ahead of time, cut out the bookmark for Luke 24:27.

Begin by giving the group members an opportunity to recite the memory verse from the previous bookmark (John 20:31). When they are finished, distribute the Luke 24:27 bookmark and have them read the verse aloud several times. Explain that this session's memory verse tells us that the whole Bible centers on the story of Jesus Christ. From start to finish, it's about what He did to make a way for us to be forgiven and saved.

Before you dismiss the group, remind students of their daily Bible reading challenge. If they haven't been reading at all, encourage them to start today. Close in prayer, asking for God's grace to work in the lives of students.

REFLECT

The following short devotions are for the students to reflect on and answer during the week. You can make a copy of these pages and distribute them to your class or download and print them from **www.gospellight.com/uncommon/jh_ the_armor_of_god.zip**.

1—LIGHT FOR YOUR PATH

Read Psalm 119:105 and turn on the light.

Through the work of the Holy Spirit, God uses His Word to give us understanding and guide our lives—but we have to quiet down and sit still long enough for the Spirit to speak! So try this: Before you start reading your Bible today, sit in silence for a minute. When the minute is up, pray something like this: "Spirit of God, open my heart to receive Your guidance. Help me to sense Your presence and direction as I meditate on Your Word. Amen."

Now read through Psalm 119:105 slowly, at least twice. When you're done, sit for another minute in silence. Then pray, "Keep my mind and heart alert today, Lord, for opportunities to put Your Word into practice. Speak to me through the events and encounters that come my way and call to my mind the wisdom I have read in Your Word. Amen."

Is it hard for you to sit still and silent? Why or why not?

_____
_____
_____

Have you ever felt God's Spirit guiding you through His Word? If so, what happened?

_____
_____
_____

2—RULES CAN BE GOOD

Check out Psalm 119:20.

Marco lives with his mom, older sister, Mandy, and baby sister, Minnie. His mom works a lot. Mandy is supposed to take care of her younger siblings, but that's not how it works out.

Instead, Mandy takes off with her boyfriend as soon as Marco gets home from school, leaving him to feed, change and play with Minnie, who is only two years old. By the time he gets the baby to sleep around 8:30 PM, he barely has time to make dinner for himself and get his homework done—and he never has time to hang out with friends or go to youth group. Marco has told his mom about Mandy leaving, but his older sister ignores everything his mom says and just does whatever she wants.

Sometimes rules are a drag, but, as this story shows, that is not always true. What does Marco's family actually need?

- ❑ No rules
- ❑ Fewer rules
- ❑ More rules
- ❑ Better rules that are followed and enforced

Do you think the person who wrote Psalm 119:20 might have been in a situation similar to Marco's, where a lack of rules made him feel insecure and exhausted? Why or why not?

_____

_____

_____

How can rules help us to understand what we should be doing?

_____

_____

_____

3—FREEDOM TO RUN

Run on over to Psalm 119:30-32.

Shandi *loves* to run. She runs cross-country for her middle school, is in a running club, and is looking forward to competing at the state level when she gets to high school. The only thing Shandi doesn't like about cross-country is when she runs a new course for the first time. Sometimes the courses aren't marked very clearly and it's easy, when she's in the "zone," to miss a turn and go the wrong way. Not only does that kind of mistake eat into her time, but getting lost in a town she's never been in is also scary!

Does Shandi have more or less freedom when the path is clearly marked? Explain your answer.

_____

_____

_____

The psalmist says in today's verses that he can "run in the path of [God's] commands." How are God's commands like markers on a cross-country course?

_____

_____

_____

How has the Bible shown you the way to go in a situation?

_____

_____

_____

4—HIDE IT IN YOUR HEART

Don't hide! Read Psalm 119:11. When Jesus met the two men on the road to Emmaus, He explained how everything they had read in the Old Testament had come to pass in His death and resurrection. These men knew the Bible because they had studied it and taken it to heart. However, they didn't understand how everything they had read pointed to Jesus.

When you memorize Bible verses, you carry the Word with you wherever you go. Does memorizing Scripture come easy to you, or is it hard? Why?

_____

_____

_____

Why is it so important to know the Bible—both the Old and New Testament?

_____

_____

_____

Ask God to help you wield the sword of the Spirit, the Bible, each day so that you can stand against the attacks of the enemy.

THE BIBLE IS THE LIVING WORD OF GOD

THE BIG IDEA

The Bible is truly a great weapon in our spiritual arsenal, and it will come alive when we realize who it's from and what it means.

SESSION AIMS

In this session, you will guide students to (1) see the Bible for what it really is— a message from the true and living God; (2) accept the Bible's authority and seek to obey its teachings; and (3) open their hearts to pursue a deeper knowledge of God through daily Bible reading.

THE BIGGEST VERSE

"Do not let this Book of the Law depart from your mouth; meditate on it day and night, so that you may be careful to do everything written in it. Then you will be prosperous and successful" (Joshua 1:8).

OTHER IMPORTANT VERSES

Nehemiah 8:3-18; Proverbs 4:23; John 1:14; Philippians 4:8; Titus 2:11; James 1:22

Note: Additional options and worksheets in 8$^1/_2$" x 11" format for this session are available for download at **www.gospellight.com/uncommon/jh_the_armor_of_god.zip**.

STARTER

Option 1: Tent Assembly. For this option, you will need your Bible and three unassembled tents (the kind that don't have to be secured to the ground with spikes). Ahead of time, make sure the tents have all their pieces. Students will be racing to assemble them.

Welcome students to this final session on the armor of God. Explain that to-day we will be concluding this study on the sword of the Spirit, which is the Word of God, and how each of us can wield it effectively in spiritual battle. Ask for a few volunteers to share something from their personal Bible reading and how they have used the Bible this week to overcome a temptation or choose to do the right thing.

Divide students into three groups and give each a tent. Instruct the group members that at your signal, they are to race to see which team can put up their tent the quickest. (Note: This might be a good thing to videotape for par-ent night—or future blackmail!) Acknowledge the winning team with a round of applause, and then let the other teams complete their tents. Allow students to sit in the tents (flaps open, thank you) throughout this session as long as they are paying attention.

Explain that the group might be wondering why we started this session off by building tents. Well, if they remember, the Jews were a nomadic people. This means that they lived in tents and traveled around a lot until they settled into the Promised Land. Our Bible story today deals with a time when the Jews had just come back from captivity and were settling into their homes again. During this homecoming, an important event happened—an eight-day church service, during which all the people camped out to hear the Word of God. Let's open the Book and find out what happened.

Option 2: Mini-Olympics. For this option, you need a Bible, music from the opening ceremony of the Olympics and "The Star-Spangled Banner," a way to play this music to the group, three towels, three water bottles, a tape measure, a table, three pies, three cans of soda, a stopwatch (or other timekeeping de-vice), a gold medal, a silver medal and a bronze medal (available at toy stores or craft stores, or you can make your own). Ahead of time, use the masking tape to make a starting and finishing line on the floor. Place the pies on the table.

Greet students and welcome them to this session on the armor of God. Ex-plain that today they will be continuing to examine the sword of the Spirit, which is the Word of God, and how they can wield it effectively. Ask for volun-teers to share something from what they have read, such as a story, a particular verse, or whatever they remember. Encourage this kind of participation from students—who knows, you might even learn something from them!

Begin by announcing to the group that you are going to start off the session with a series of contests that will demonstrate their skill, discipline and supreme athletic ability. Choose three volunteers to compete as athletes in this mini-Olympic competition. Have the volunteers come forward, and give them each a water bottle and a towel. Choose three more volunteers to come forward and be the coaches for the three athletes. Play the opening ceremony music as the volunteers get ready to compete with some stretching and warm-up exercises. (Encourage the coaches to do their job of ranting, raving, and so on.)

Run the athletes through the following games, awarding three points to the person who comes in first, two points to the person who comes in second, and one point to the person who comes in third:

- *Cartwheel Run*: Have athletes cartwheel as fast as they can from the starting taped line to the finish line.
- *Flamingo Competition*: Have the athletes place their hands on their heads and see who can stand on one leg the longest.
- *Pie-eating Contest*: Have students place their hands behind their backs and eat as much pie as possible in three minutes.
- *Burping Contest*: Give each athlete a can of soda. At your signal, have them drink for 15 seconds. Signal a stop, and then see which one can produce the loudest burp.
- *Headstand Competition*: Have the students get into a headstand position and see who can stay up the longest.

At the end of the games, total the points and declare a winner. Play the national anthem and have a medal ceremony to place the gold, silver and bronze medals on the athletes.

Conclude by sharing that contests are always interesting—those who can do things faster, better or longer than others are always fascinating. Next, ask the students who they think could read the Bible the longest if you were to have a contest. How many hours could they read it without falling asleep? Let the students respond.

Sum up by explaining that today you want to talk about a church service that could possibly have won a gold medal for the longest in history. The people at that service weren't falling asleep, however. What made the difference? Why were people so involved? Let's open the Book and find out.

MESSAGE

Option 1: Toolbox. For this option, you will need several Bibles, adult helpers, a toolbox with different types of tools (hammer, screwdriver, level, tape measure, ruler, carpenter's pencil, wrench—whatever you have handy), four hammers, a box of 16 penny nails, four paper bags, a sheet of plywood, and four 2 x 4s. Ahead of time, lean the plywood against a wall so that it is tilted at an angle that is safe for students and the wall behind it. Have adult helpers hold it steady during the option. Place the 2 x 4s at the foot of the plywood. Put about 10 nails into each of the four paper bags.

Begin by stating that you hope during this series the group has learned more about the Bible and what it really is than they knew before. The one thing you hope they will remember is that the purpose of the Bible is to give us a way to know God and understand His plan for our lives so we can stand strong against the enemy. When we read the Bible, we are using this tool that God has given to build a life that is solid and strong—a life connected to Him.

Show students the toolbox filled with tools and hold each item up one by one, explaining for what each is used. Explain that a carpenter wouldn't just sit and look at these tools; he would use them to build something. Hold up your Bible and explain that this is the way the Bible is meant to be used. It is a tool for knowing God. To get the full benefit of this tool, we need to read it daily. As with any tool, the more we use it, the easier it will become for us to use.

Have adult helpers stationed at the plywood to ensure students are following instructions. Choose 16 volunteers and have them break into four groups of four. Have the groups all line up facing the large sheet of plywood. Give each group a hammer and a bag of nails. Before you begin, stress that this is not a race and that the students need to be very careful. Then have one student from each group go to the plywood and, as a group, nail one of the 2 x 4s to the plywood horizontally. This will take a little bit of teamwork.

When the groups are finished, you should end up with a long strip of wood parallel to the floor. Have the next four students (one from each group) come

Youth Leader Tip

Let your group members know that you really believe the Bible is God's Word! Your solid conviction and simple instruction will go a long way in helping students open their hearts to the Lord.

forward and nail the next 2 x 4 to the plywood. Continue until all the groups have gone.

When this is finished, ask the students what would have happened if you had asked the volunteers to nail the 2 x 4s to the plywood, but hadn't given them any tools to do it. (*The answer would be that they wouldn't have been able to accomplish the task.*) Explain that in the same way, God has given us a tool—His Word, the Bible—to enable us to know Him and understand His plan for our lives.

Distribute Bibles and have students follow along as you read Nehemiah 7:73–8:18. (This is a long passage so practice first or you might put students to sleep!) When you are fished, explain that the Israelites had just returned to their homeland after being held as slaves in a foreign country for many years. As they settled back into the cities, one of the first things they did was to get out the Word of God and read it again. This passage talks about one of the longest church services ever—hours and hours of Bible reading, but no one fell asleep. They listened attentively, wept and rejoiced.

Explain that the Israelites knew that it was their neglect of God's Word that had caused them to be taken captive in the first place. Now that they were back in their homeland, they wanted to do things right. So Ezra, the priest, read the words of the Law to the people and the leaders explained it all to them. Then the Israelites celebrated for eight days.

Continue by stating that the Word of God was not just a religious book to those recently returned Jews—it was their joy and their strength, because they recognized that it was that Word that gave them a way to know their Deliverer personally. The same holds true for us. The Bible is a tool from God so that we can know Him. When we read it, opening our hearts to accept its authority into our lives, God can use it to speak to us and to shape our lives into something that honors and glorifies Him.

Option 2: Feeling Sleepy? For this option, you will need several Bibles, a reclining chair, chamomile tea, a tea cup, hot water, reading glasses, a thick and dusty book, soft music, a way to play the music for the group, a candle, matches, a blanket and a pillow. Ahead of time, set up the recliner facing the students. Have the music ready to play for the group. Make a cup of hot chamomile tea.

Begin a discussion by the group members about what makes them sleepy. (*Some ideas might include reading, riding in a car for a long time, eating a big meal, and so on.*) Explain that you have brought some things with you that always make you sleepy. Choose a volunteer to come forward and invite him or her to sit in the recliner. Give the volunteer the cup of tea, pillow and blanket. Dim the room lights and light the candle. Turn on the soft music and hand the volunteer the book and reading glasses.

After the volunteer has been made as comfortable as possible, ask the students how long they think it will take for the volunteer to fall asleep. Depending on the volunteer, the answer could be anywhere from 2 seconds to 30 minutes. Let the volunteer stay up front as you discuss the following questions with the group:

- What's the fastest you've ever fallen asleep?
- Where's the oddest place you've fallen asleep?
- Have you ever seen anyone fall asleep during church? (*You'll probably get a few great stories!*)
- How long was the longest church service you've ever attended?
- What happened during the service?
- Did you stay interested the whole time?

Transition by stating that you would now like to read a story about an extremely long church service. As we read this story from the book of Nehemiah, we will find out who fell asleep during this service. Distribute Bibles and read aloud Nehemiah 7:73–8:18. (This is a long passage, so rehearse your reading first or *you* might put students to sleep!) When you have finished, explain that the Israelites had just returned to their homeland after being held as slaves in a foreign country for many years. As they settled back into their cities, one of the first things they did was get out the Word of God and read it again. This passage talks about one of the longest church services ever—hours and hours of Bible reading—but *no one* feel asleep. Have students refer back to the passage, and then discuss the following questions:

- Who was assembled in the square to hear the Word? (*Men, women and all who were able to understand [verse 2].*)
- Who read the law to them? (*Ezra, the priest [verse 2].*)
- How long did Ezra read from the Law? (*From sunrise to noon [verse 3].*)
- How did the people listen to the Word? (*Attentively [verse 3].*)
- What was the people's response to the reading of the Word of God? (*They praised God and worshiped Him [verse 6].*)[1]
- How did the Levites (priests) help out as the Law was being read? (*They explained it to the people [verses 7-8].*)

- Why do you think the people wept at the reading of the law? (*Possibilities might include because they were overjoyed at having the Word available to them again, they were repentant, and so on.*)
- What did Nehemiah tell the people to do? (*To go eat and celebrate [verse 10].*)
- How long did the celebration last? (*Eight days [verse 18].*)

Ask the group if they could imagine reading the Bible and celebrating the Word of God with other Christians for more than a week. (*Probably not.*) However, the Israelites realized what a treasure the Word of God truly was. We have this Word available to us as well—and it has been made even clearer by the coming of Jesus Christ, the Living Word. The Bible is an inspired message from God, and as we read it, we discover more and more of what God is like and what His plans are for our lives.

DIG

Option 1: Joshua 1:8 Challenge. For this option, you will need several Bibles, contemporary worship music, a way to play it for the group, copies of "Joshua 1:8 Challenge" (found on the next page), and pens or pencils.

Ask the group members to name their favorite Bible verse and tell a little bit about why they like it. Usually, Bible verses are the most meaningful to us when they have somehow helped us understand God and His plan better—either by comforting us or giving us guidance and direction. Ask the students how the verse has touched their lives personally.

Distribute the "Joshua 1:8 Challenge" and pens or pencils to the group. Tell the students to find a quiet place in the room where they will be able to think and fill out the worksheet on their own. Explain that you are going to give them about 10 minutes to answer the questions, and then you will call them back to discuss their responses as a group. As the students work through

Youth Leader Tip
Try to avoid a strickly teacher/student relationship and instead approach the material as two learners. When you and the group study together, the atmosphere will be more conducive for learning.[2]

JOSHUA 1:8 CHALLENGE

Look up Joshua 1:8 and write it out below.

_____

_____

According to this verse, what are we *not* supposed to do?

_____

_____

What *are* we supposed to do?

_____

_____

What will happen if we follow this advice?

_____

_____

Is there anything that keeps you from reading the Bible? If so, what?

_____

_____

What could you do to change this?

_____

_____

_____

What goal would you like to set for yourself as far as your daily Bible reading?

_____

_____

_____

What goal would you like to make for your yearly Bible reading?

_____

_____

the handout, play some worship music in the background to help create a sense of privacy and keep them more focused.

When the 10 minutes are up, call the group back together and discuss each of the responses:

1. Look up Joshua 1:8 and write it out below. (*"Do not let this Book of the Law depart from your mouth; meditate on it day and night, so that you may be careful to do everything written in it. Then you will be prosperous and successful."*)
2. According to this verse, what are we *not* supposed to do? (*Let the Book of the Law depart from our mouths.*)
3. What *are* we supposed to do? (*Meditate on the words of the Bible day and night.*)
4. What will happen if we follow this advice? (*We will be prosperous and successful.*)
5. Is there anything that keeps you from reading the Bible? If so, what? (*Let students share their answers. If they are intimidated, share some of the things you have struggled with regarding consistent Bible reading.*)
6. What could you do to change this? (*Suggest some answers to each of the problems shared in the above question.*)
7. What goal would you like to set for yourself as far as your daily Bible reading? (*Challenge every student to answer, even if it's a verse a day.*)
8. What goal would you like to make for your yearly Bible reading? (*Again, challenge every student to answer something. Commitment starts with a decision.*)

Conclude by explaining that just as we read today from Nehemiah 8, the Word of God is much more than a book. It is like having a face-to-face conversation with God. When we read the Bible, we allow God to speak His wisdom and guidance into our lives and comfort us. Realizing this truth can increase our hunger for the Word of God and keep us diligent about reading it daily.

Option 2: Mull It Over. For this option, you will need this story. Read aloud the following to the group:

Jana began listening to the brand-new music she had just bought and sank deep into her favorite beanbag chair. She grabbed her favorite magazine and flipped open to the latest article about finding the boyfriend of her dreams. With music pumping, she meandered through the ads and advice, thinking about how she could use what she had read to hook Jake, the sophomore JV soccer star, for her area league. Closing her eyes, she mulled over what she had read until her thoughts were interrupted by a call to come downstairs for dinner. Breathing out a sigh, she dog-eared the corner of the article and headed down to the table, still thinking over the words she had read.

Ask the students if any of them have ever read an article and thought about it over and over again, trying to figure out how they could use what they had read. Explain that when we mull ideas over in our minds, we are *meditating* on those words. The Bible tells us to meditate on God's Word day and night. Why? Because when we do, we give the Holy Spirit the opportunity to change us and make us more like Jesus.

Have the students read Romans 12:2 and Joshua 1:8. Discuss the following:

- What comes to mind when you think of "meditating" on something? (*Let students respond.*)
- On what was Jana meditating? (*Teen magazine boyfriend advice.*)
- Was this the most beneficial thing she could be thinking about? (*Nope. God has much more accurate advice about love, life and dating.*)
- Why is it important to be careful about what you meditate on or think about? (*Proverbs 4:23 says that we should guard our hearts because from it flows our very life. What we store up in our hearts will be a driving force behind the kind of life path we take.*)
- What did God give us to meditate on? (*His very Word, which is full of life, truth and wisdom.*)
- How can meditating on God's Word benefit us in daily life? (*Having God's perspective on life helps us to honor Him in our choices.*)
- Does this mean we should only think about the Bible? (*No, but everything we do should be weighed against it—whether that's friendships, school decisions, church involvement or entertainment. As a Christ-follower, we wouldn't want anything less than His will, right?*)

Conclude by rereading Joshua 1:8. Challenge the group members to always be working on memorizing a verse, as this will help keep them diligent about meditating on the Word of God. Also encourage them to keep their minds set on God, as this will keep their lives moving in the right direction.

APPLY

Option 1: Now Is the Time. For this option, you will need the power of the Holy Spirit working in the hearts of the students—so pray hard!

Explain that the words "reliable," "accurate" and "indestructible" are all descriptions we have applied to the Bible during this series. God has given us the Bible so we can know Him and understand His plan for our lives. The Bible is an incredible gift, *but* it is not an end in and of itself. It is meant to point us to an intimate knowledge of God—a real relationship with Him.

Read Titus 2:11 and John 1:14. State that if anyone has never opened his or her heart to God and accepted His gift of salvation, now is the time. Lead students in a time of repentance and salvation as the Holy Spirit directs you. You can pray over the group, have them pray for each other, or have them come forward for personal prayer with adult leaders. Whatever method you choose, end by encouraging the group members to commit to reading the Bible daily.

Option 2: Bookmark Memory Verses 3. This is a continuation of option 2 from sessions 8–11. You will need a copy of the "Bookmark Memory Verses" sheet you previously created. Ahead of time, cut out the bookmark for Joshua 1:8.

Begin by giving the group members an opportunity to recite the memory verse from the previous bookmark (Luke 24:27). When they are finished, distribute the Joshua 1:8 bookmark and have them read the verse aloud several times. Explain that this is the last memory verse from this series and that it hopefully will serve as a reminder to them for many years to come of the importance of God's Word. Remind the group that the Bible can impact every part of our lives if we let it. Our job is to read it and obey it, and in doing so, God will order our steps and cause us to be blessed and like Him. This doesn't mean we will have a problem-free life, but a life of God's grace and guidance.

Before you dismiss the group, remind students of their daily Bible reading challenge. If they haven't been reading, encourage them to start today. Close in prayer, asking for God's blessing and grace to work in their lives.

Youth Leader Tip

Young believers can be easily sidetracked from their walk with God. To help prevent this, offer a discipleship group for students who are new in their faith. This group could meet before your regular youth service or other time you feel is convenient.

REFLECT

The following short devotions are for the students to reflect on and answer during the week. You can make a copy of these pages and distribute them to your class or download and print them from **www.gospellight.com/uncommon/jh_the_armor_of_god.zip**.

1—WORD MADE FLESH

Who came from the Father? Find out in John 1:14. The Bible is incredible for many reasons. It tells the story of God's actions in human history, guides our desire to live godly lives, and shows us the future God has planned. But the *most* incredible thing about Scripture is that it reveals Jesus Christ, the Word sent from God to become one of us and to make us a part of His family. God's Word, the Bible, leads us to know and love the Living Word, Jesus.

Jesus faced temptation and doubt just like us. How does it feel to know that the God we worship is not just "out there" but has felt tired and sad, angry and hurt—just like you?

_____

_____

_____

Jesus faced every kind of temptation, but He did so without sinning. Romans 8:11 tells us, "If the Spirit of him who raised Jesus from the dead is living in you, he who raised Christ from the dead will also give life to your mortal bodies because of his Spirit who lives in you." When you ask Jesus to be Lord of your life, the Holy Spirit walks with you every day, ready to guide your words, actions and thoughts. Write a short prayer thanking the Holy Spirit for His presence. Ask Him to keep you alert to His guidance as you face your day!

_____

_____

_____

2—THINK ABOUT SUCH THINGS

Think about this: Philippians 4:8.

Tanya is so excited for the sleepover at Vera's on Friday night. Vera is the coolest girl in eighth grade, and Tanya still can't believe she got an invitation!

But a few minutes after her dad drops her off, Tanya wishes the invitation never came. Vera's plan is for the girls to watch all of the *Saw* slasher movies, one after another, all night long. Tanya knows her dad would never give her permission to watch R-rated horror films, and she also knows that if she watches them, her brain will replay every obscene and violent image again and again . . .

What should Tanya do in this situation?

❑   Try to convince Vera and the girls to do something else
❑   Call her dad to pick her up
❑   Look away from the TV when things get scary or violent
❑   Watch the movies and hope she gets amnesia

Today's verse gives specific advice about the kinds of things you should let in your brain—not because you're too young or immature, but because you're trying to live a godly life. Why do you think your mind is so important to God?

_____

_____

_____

Is there anything you're putting in your mind that fails the "Philippians 4:8 Test"? List the things you need to get rid of.

_____

_____

_____

3—GOD'S PURPOSES

Fill up on Isaiah 55:11. God's promise in today's verse means that every minute you spend in His Word getting to know the Living Word, Jesus, is time He spends transforming you into the person He created you to be. Your study time might sometimes feel pointless or dry, but it's not! God's Spirit is constantly at work, whether or not you can sense it, and He will be faithful to complete His plans for your life (see Philippians 1:6).

What is one character trait (such as patience, honesty, kindness or courage) that you want to grow in this week?

_____

_____

_____

In what ways are you falling a little short in that area?

_____

_____

_____

Write a prayer asking God to work in you to form that character trait, and thank Him for His Word, which always accomplishes His purposes for your life.

_____

_____

_____

4—REJOICE!

Don't cry! Check out Nehemiah 8:9-10.

Remember the story of Nehemiah? Long ago, the ancient Israelites endured a terrible attack. Their country was torn apart when many of the survivors were carried off into exile hundreds of miles away, and Jerusalem, their capital city, was demolished. Years later, a man named Nehemiah and a man named Ezra returned to Jerusalem to help the people rebuild. But they didn't just have to rebuild the city walls or the Temple; they also had to rebuild the people's knowledge of God's Word. Most of the people who could read had been taken away, so the rest had not heard Scripture read aloud for many years. The younger ones had *never* heard it!

So Nehemiah and Ezra gathered the people together for a reading of God's Word. When the people heard it, many of them wept! They were so moved by the gift of Scripture that they cried. But the leaders told them *not* to cry, but to rejoice and throw a party instead!

In our day, we have such easy access to the Bible that we can forget what a rare and precious gift it is. Imagine never being able to read God's Word again. What do you think would happen?

_____

_____

_____

You will probably always have access to a Bible, and that's a good reason to rejoice! Instead of taking it for granted, say a short prayer thanking God for the miraculous gift of His Word.

USE YOUR SWORD!

The first swords are believed to have developed around 1600 BC. In the beginning these were nothing more than just elongated bronze daggers, but as time went by smiths began to refine them and add crossguards and other features that we find on swords today. By the time of Paul, iron swords were common.

The typical Roman sword was known as a *gladius.* It was the Roman soldier's primary weapon for close, hand-to-hand combat (they carried javelins and darts for long-range attacks), and often his last line of defense if his life was in danger. The Roman gladius had a two-edged blade and a tapered point for stabbing. A Roman soldier typically crashed into his enemy with his shield, hopefully knocking him off balance, and then followed up with a sword thrust. The soldier could attack and be protected as long as he stayed behind his shield.

Roman soldiers trained relentlessly for battle. They fought with wooden swords in full battle armor and practiced for hours each day. Roman soldiers were trained to fight hard and improvise in battle when needed to get an advantage over the enemy. They travelled and fought together in groups of eight. During a battle, it was easy for soldiers to get tired (they carried around about 60 pounds of equipment), so the Romans devised a strategy whereby one soldier would fight at the front of the column for 15 minutes, and then move to the back. The soldiers were close to each other and depended on one another. They also depended on their generals and leaders for battle tactics and to encourage them in the fight.

Although swords fell out of use after the advent of gunpowder during the Middle Ages, it is still an effective metaphor for how we are to use the Word of God. Like the Roman soldier, we are to go into battle against our enemy fully equipped and use our sword to damage his kingdom of darkness. The Bible is "sharper than any double-edged sword" (Hebrews 4:12), and the truth of what we find therein can destroy the lies of the enemy.

Of course, to use the sword effectively, we have to train, which is where Bible study and memorizing Scriptures come in. Just like the Roman soldiers, we need to be prepared for battle and not only ready to defend ourselves but also ready to go on the offensive and attack. This is exactly what Jesus did when Satan tempted Him in the wilderness in Luke 4. Whenever the devil went on the offensive with a temptation, Jesus parried his attacks by quoting Scripture. As James 4:7 tells us, "Resist the devil, and he will flee from you." A good way for us to resist is to equip the sword of the Spirit and strike back against the enemy's assaults.

Notice that Roman soldiers depended on each other. In this battle, we are never alone. God has given us many other Christians that are in the same battle, and we can gain support and strength from them. When we grow weary in the fight, we can turn to these individuals for help. Even more important, we can turn to God, our commander, for wisdom and we can rely on His power for strength. When we do this and wield our sword effectively, we will ultimately gain the victory!

ENDNOTES

Session 1

1. Moses made a similar challenge in Exodus 32 after the Israelites sinned by creating a golden calf and worshiping it. He told the people, "Whoever is for the LORD, come to me" (verse 26). The Levites rallied to him, and then they went through the camp and killed all those who had not crossed to Moses' side of the line.

Session 2

1. Paul's description here is most likely drawn from the depiction of the heavenly warrior in Isaiah 59:17: "He put on righteousness as his breastplate, and the helmet of salvation on his head; he put on the garments of vengeance and wrapped himself in zeal as in a cloak." As theologian N.T. Wright states, "The basic meaning of 'righteousness' and its cognates. . . denotes not so much the abstract idea of justice or virtue as right standing and consequent right behaviour within a community." See David F. Wright, Sinclair Ferguson and J.I. Packer (eds.), *New Dictionary of Theology* (Downers Grove, IL: IVP, 1988), pp. 590-592.

Session 3

1. There are two ways to interpret the Greek word translated as "readiness" (*hetoimasia*). The one that best fits the context of this verse is in the sense of a "prepared foundation," which gives the meaning that "the knowledge of the dependence on *the gospel* that gives a person *peace* in heart and life is a necessary *equipment* (like the hobnailed sandals of the Roman soldier)." Francis Foulkes, "Ephesians," *Tyndale New Testament Commentaries* (Grand Rapids, MI: Wm. B. Eerdmans, 1989), p. 182.

Session 4

1. The Greek word for "shield" (*thyreos*) comes from the word for "door" and implies covering the entire body. Interestingly, in 1 Thessalonians 5:8 Paul uses a different piece of spiritual armor for faith: "But since we belong to the day, let us be self-controlled, putting on faith and love as a breastplate, and the hope of salvation as a helmet."

Session 5

1. One site is http://dictionary.reference.com/etymology.
2. The Greek word for "salvation" is *soteria*, meaning "deliverance, preservation, safety." The Hebrew word is *yasha*, meaning "to save, be saved, be delivered." Psalm 140:7 provides a strong parallel to this verse: "O Sovereign Lord, my strong deliverer, who shields my head in the day of battle."

Session 6

1. While prayer cannot quite be described as part of the armor of God, it is nonetheless an important compent of the Christian's success in standing against the enemy. The New Testament frequently directs believers not to cease in prayer (see Luke 18:1; Romans 12:12; Philippians 4:6; Colossians 4:5; 1 Thessalonians 5:17), and here the point is that every aspect of life should be delt with in prayer.
2. Jim Burns, *Uncommon Youth Ministry* (Ventura, CA: Gospel Light, 2007), p. 116.

Unit I Conclusion

1. Tom Bowman, "Body Armor Saves 'Lucky' Marine in Iraq," NPR, October 6, 2006. http://www.npr.org/templates/story/story.php?storyId=6206046.
2. C. J. Chivers, "Sniper Attacks Adding to Peril of U.S. Troops," *The New York Times,* November 4, 2006. http://www.nytimes.com/2006/11/04/world/middleeast/04sniper.html?pagewanted=2.

Session 7

1. To clarify some terms used in this unit, "revelation" refers to God's self-disclosure. God reveals Himself to us in both general ways (nature) and specific ways (His Word). "Inspiration" is the process by which God guided the writers of the Scriptures so that they wrote the words He wanted. "Illumination" refers to the work of the Holy Spirit to give understanding of the Word that God has revealed.

Session 8

1. In speaking of 2 Timothy 3:16, theologian Benjamin Warfield said, "The Greek word *theopneustos* [inspired] . . . does not mean 'inspired of God.' . . . [it has] nothing to say of inspiring or inspiration: it speaks only of 'spiring or 'spiration.' What it says of Scripture is, not that it is 'breathed into by God' or is the product of the Divine 'inbreathing,' into its human authors, but that it is breathed out by God, 'God-breathed,' the product of the creative breath of God." See Benjamin Warfield, *The Inspiration and Authority of the Bible* (Philadelphia, PA: The Presbyterian Reformed Publishing Company, 1948), pp. 132-133.

Session 9

1. In AD 64 a great fire broke out in Rome, and Nero was rumored to have started it himself. To get rid of the report, Nero used the Christians as a scapegoat, effectively captalizing on the Roman public's existing suspicion of this group. Christians were burned, crucified and fed to wild animals during his reign. The persecutions continued until the time of Julian the Apostate, who in AD 363 attempted to restore paganism to the Roman empire.

Session 10

1. According to Norman Geisler and William Nix, "The word *testament,* which is better translated 'covenant,' is taken from the Hebrew and Greek words designating a compact or agreement between two parties. In the case of the Bible, then, we have the old contract between God and His people, the Jews, and the new compact between God and Christians. Christian scholars have stressed the unity between these two Testaments of the Bible in terms of the person of Jesus Christ who claimed to be its unifying theme. St. Augustine said the New Testament is veiled in the Old Testament, and the Old Testament is unveiled in the New Testament. . . . Christ is enfolded in the Old Testament, but unfolded it the New." See Norman Geisler and William Nix, *From God to Us* (Chicago: Moody Press, 1974), pp. 7-8.

Session 11

1. Be careful not to imply that the Bible *becomes* the Word of God when you understand it. This neo-orthodox viewpoint is not in line with traditional Christian teachings. The Bible is a divine revelation from God; it doesn't take our understanding of it to make it His Word. The act of illumination, when the Holy Spirit brings understanding to us, changes us, not the Word. The Bible is what it is—the eternal and indestructible Word of the one true God.

Session 12

1. The word "worship" used in Nehemiah 8:6 literally means "to prostrate oneself on the ground." Such reverence and awe for God and His Word drew not just a celebratory response from the Israelites, but a "holy moment" of awe as well. This profound sense of worship comes when our souls brush against the holiness of God—and it changes us forever. We can cultivate it in students by giving a place for silent reflection and adoration in each meeting. Don't rush to fill each moment with sound. Silence can speak volumes when it is a response of worship before an awesome and mighty God.
2. Jim Burns, *Uncommon Youth Ministry* (Ventura, CA: Gospel Light, 2005), p. 108.